TRAILER TRASH
FROM TENNESSEE

Other Books by David Hunter

THE MOON IS ALWAYS FULL
BLACK FRIDAY COMING DOWN
THE JIGSAW MAN
THERE WAS BLOOD ON THE SNOW
THE NIGHT IS MINE
HOMICIDE GAME

TRAILER TRASH FROM TENNESSEE

DAVID HUNTER

RUTLEDGE HILL PRESS
Nashville, Tennessee

This book is the story of my childhood as remembered through the mists of more than thirty-five years. Real names have been used where I could remember them and do so without embarrassing anyone. I have used composite characters and time compression in some instances for the sake of brevity.

Published in Nashville, Tennessee, by Rutledge Hill Press, 211 Seventh Avenue North, Nashville, Tennessee 37219.

Typography by E. T. Lowe Publishing Co., Nashville, Tennessee.

Library of Congress Cataloging-in-Publication Data

Hunter, David, 1947–
    Trailer trash from Tennessee / David Hunter.
      p. cm.
    ISBN 1-55853-346-X
    1. Tennessee, East—Social life and customs. 2. Hunter, David,
    1947– —Childhood and youth. 3. Tennessee, East—Biography.
    I. Title.
    F442.1.H86   1995
    976.8'053'092—dc20
    [B]   95-2675
                                               CIP

Printed in the United States of America.

1 2 3 4 5 6 7 8 9 — 99 98 97 96 95

This book is for my father, William Henry Hunter, who did not live to see his first grandchild. He taught me things I never knew I was learning.

Contents

TRAILER TRASH FROM TENNESSEE

Foreword

*T*HE ART OF cartoonist Bill Watterson has spoken to my heart since the first time I read one of his *Calvin and Hobbes* strips on the comic page of my hometown paper. In fact, he speaks not only to me, but also to my son—and on the exact same level. When the two of us read *Calvin and Hobbes* together, the thirty-three years' difference in our ages means nothing.

Boys of a tender age take heart from Calvin's apparent lack of fear of the giants in the adult world, and boys in their forties remember when they were still as brave as Calvin and sure of their ability to face the world on their own terms.

Calvin is a rambunctious boy of six, with a jaundiced eye toward society and a determination to live life to the fullest. He is aided and abetted by Hobbes, his faithful confidant, who just happens to be a tiger.

To everyone else—adults, girls, and even little boys without imagination—Hobbes is merely a stuffed animal. To Calvin, and to those of a like spirit, Hobbes is very real: a strong, confident, and wise creature, the perfect companion for a small boy. Calvin, unfettered by dull reality, embarks upon journeys and adventures his imagination-impaired colleagues cannot begin to grasp.

Calvin does not *pretend*, he *lives* his adventures, whether it

11

means climbing a child's slide as tall as the Washington Monument or fighting disgusting alien slugs in the far reaches of the universe. Calvin does not surrender to the mundane, the common.

All great writers, I believe, manage to hang on to the magic of childhood and imagination. I can think of no better example than Mark Twain.

Remember the scene in *Huckleberry Finn* where Huck and Tom Sawyer, in the best tradition of high adventure, decide to free Jim from the building where he is being held captive?

Tom's original literary and heroic intent is to dig a tunnel with case knives, pretending that the process is taking place over a thirty-eight-year span of time. When it quickly becomes evident that the case knives are not a viable option as digging tools, Tom decides—for reasons of practicality—to use real digging tools.

To Huck's utter confusion, however, and in direct defiance of conventional thought, Tom then tells his companion to hand him a case knife. When the practical and unassuming Huck hands him one, Tom glares and once more emphatically demands a *case knife*. Finally catching on, Huck hands him a pickax, with which he immediately begins to dig.

To one possessed of an imagination such as Tom Sawyer's, a thing had to be done in compliance with the rules of whatever imaginary adventure was in progress at the time. Or in Tom's words, "It don't make no difference how foolish it is, it's the *right* way—and it's the regular way."

That scene was obviously a parable about the power of romantic imagination over grim reality—at least to young boys like me and Mark Twain.

The mind of a boy is a wonderful place, full of endless, exotic adventures. I have done my best to recapture that feeling on the pages of this book.

In some places, the reader will have to slip with me back and forth between realities. Is it Sergeant Preston of the Yukon confronting a maddened bull, or a small boy by the name of David trying to take a cow home from the pasture?

Is it Prince Valiant on a crusade to rid the world of unchival-rous scoundrels, or a runny-nosed child fighting for street survival in a South Carolina trailer park in 1952?

If you want to know, come with me on a grand adventure. Walk with me through the technicolor memories of my childhood, the times when I too could conjure up tigers like Bill Watterson's Hobbes, fight Mongol hordes on a hillside in East Tennessee, or stalk giant birds of prey on the dusty plains behind my house.

I'm ready when you are.

—1—

Never Grab
a Honeybee

*E*VERY STORY BEGINS somewhere. Mine began on Vermont Avenue in a section of North Knoxville, Tennessee, called Beaumont. The neighborhood—even in those long-ago days—was already being deserted by the more affluent. It was the first of many dwellings in which I would reside with my parents before striking out on my own some eighteen years later. I arrived in this world (some say appropriately) on April Fool's Day 1947.

We lived in a white clapboard house with black shutters, surrounded by mimosa trees. It was on a hill, as are most houses in a city where you are always climbing up or going down. I shared a fenced-in back yard with a white rabbit and a black cocker spaniel. On a screened back porch a tame pigeon lived. Eventually, a magnificent tomcat joined the menagerie and one day ate the pigeon.

I was the firstborn of my parents and the first grandchild born to my mother's parents. Of course, I was spoiled by my mother's three sisters and two brothers and saw myself as an extraordinary individual indeed.

I began talking at so young an age—and so fluently—that

one of my father's sisters predicted I would never live. I was, she said, "the only genius ever born into the family."

She was wrong, at least in her prophecy of my impending doom. As for genius . . . well, that is relative, I have found. A man who cannot balance his own checkbook without help, in my opinion, does not qualify.

My father, William Henry Hunter, came from what is today called a "disadvantaged background" and a "dysfunctional" family. The neighbors simply called them "white trash." He was in the process of escaping that type of existence when I was born. In the end, only he and his brother Emery (of all his brothers and sisters) truly escaped the grubby poverty of rented, run-down houses and alcoholic existence.

A short, powerfully built man, my father had a shock of black hair and the coloring of an Italian or Portuguese, which belied his Scots-French ancestry. He had left school, sick of poverty, to drive an ice truck at age fifteen. At eighteen, he was wading ashore at Iwo Jima with the Third Marine Division. At twenty, he returned home, determined to marry a woman totally unlike the women of his childhood.

My mother was his choice. Helen Venetta Goin, then twenty-one, was five feet, one inch tall, with raven black hair, freckles, and green eyes. She was descended from Germans on her mother's side and the dark and mysterious East Tennessee hill people called Melungeons on her father's side.

She had been raised on a farm and, even though a year older than my father, was still a naive girl who had been shielded by an overly protective family and a rural upbringing.

My father, a veteran of two bloody campaigns in the South Pacific, had to get *his* mother's permission when he married my mother in June 1946. A little less than a year later, I was born.

My earliest memories are of that fenced-in yard. I spent a lot of time playing with my pets, sometimes imagining that I was an animal trainer like the one I had seen in a movie at the Lee Theater. My cocker spaniel would become a giant wolf and the rabbit whatever beast I conjured that day. The pigeon, of course, was a bird of prey, waiting to swoop down when my back was turned.

Little of my time was spent with other children, even though there was a flock of kids one house down, crammed into a ramshackle little shanty.

I was not allowed to play with them because they reminded my father of his childhood: poor, dirty, profane, and rowdy. They probably had lice, Daddy often said. He had never recovered from the shame of once having been infested with the creatures when he was a child.

Often, while watching the boys (ranging in age from about ten to younger than myself) roam freely, I was envious. Solitary by nature, however, I could produce my own vivid, imaginary worlds, worlds in which I was king.

Sometimes, the rowdy little boys from the shack would stop and look over the fence at my pets, though they rarely acknowledged my presence. I was three when the boys were indirectly responsible for teaching me two valuable lessons involving people and honeybees.

The boys came off the hill and across the alley behind my house one sweltering summer afternoon. As they walked by, all of them were laughing uproariously. They were a group of redheaded barbarians who roamed at large. Their two-year-old brother, Teddy, tagged along behind them, wearing a diaper that, as usual, was wet and filthy.

Teddy fascinated me for two reasons: his hair had never been cut, which made him look like a little girl, and he had never spoken a word at age two. I hung on to the fence and hollered at the group of boys as they went by.

"What are y'all laughin' about?"

They disdainfully ignored me, but I persevered.

"Hey! What are y'all laughin' about?"

"Teddy picked up a bee," one of the older boys said, stopping for a moment.

"A *real* bee?"

"Yeah." I remember the boy's bare feet to this day. They were filthy and had the appearance of leather parchment.

"Did it sting him?"

"Nope," the older brother said.

"Then what are y'all laughin' about?"

"Well, if you catch a honeybee by the wings, he can't sting ya. You hold him up in the air, open your mouth, and he'll give you a drop of honey to let him go. Teddy got honey in his eye."

The barbarian looked to his multitude of brothers, winking for confirmation, and they all nodded vigorously.

I watched them head home, still laughing, followed by the silent Teddy. After a while, I wandered over to a patch of clover and watched the bees buzzing around.

As I studied them closely, what I had been told seemed plausible. As far as I could tell, the portion of the bee's anatomy that did the stinging was on the opposite side from the wings, and everyone knows that bees do produce honey. I decided to try it.

Suddenly I became an intrepid hunter, stalking a giant winged monster through the forest of clover and dandelions.

It took me a while to find a cooperative bee, but finally I found one that was not as cautious as the others. Carefully reaching down, in deep concentration, I seized the monster by its wings.

Moments later a jolt of pain ran up my arm. It was the first pain I ever remember. The intrepid hunter evaporated as the shock wave roared up my arm and connected with my brain.

Hurtling across the yard, screaming at the top of my lungs, trying to shake the beast loose, I was met by my frightened mother at the back porch.

As cold water was running over my hand, I sobbed out the story of the treacherous lie that had been told me. Fighting back her own laughter, my mother bandaged wet cigarette tobacco (supposedly a cure for stings) over the wound.

I still remember what my father said that afternoon. He never had to repeat it. It is emblazoned across my consciousness even today.

"Son," he said, "from now on, remember: never grab a honeybee, and don't believe *everything* people tell you."

I never did find out what the redheaded barbarians were really laughing about that day.

——2——

The Iceman Cometh

*M*EMORIES ARE NOT chronological; they are selective. From time to time, certain events become entangled inseparably, for no particular reason, and have no real connection except in memory. I, for instance, never see a toy fire engine without thinking of icemen and iceboxes.

For the tender memories of younger readers, an icebox was the device for keeping food cool before the refrigerator was in wide use. Shocking, isn't it? Most people living in the free world today can't imagine that there was a time when there were no refrigerators.

The widespread use of refrigeration not only changed the habits of grocery shoppers within my relatively short lifetime, but also did away with iceboxes and the old and honored profession of iceman, once as common a calling as the door-to-door milkman, who also virtually vanished from American neighborhoods in the course of a generation.

An icebox was simplicity itself: it was an enclosed, insulated box with a door on the front. Underneath the cooling compartment was a tray where chunks of ice were placed. The ice, of course, melted and the water was caught in a pan placed underneath. Every other day or so the iceman delivered more ice.

He wore a uniform similar to that of the milkman. It was white with a hat like those worn by police and bus drivers today, with a hard, shiny bill and a peaked top. The iceman was an artist at what he did. His tools were the tongs and the ice pick. Yes, there *was* once a genuine use for ice picks other than as murder weapons in scary movies. The ice pick was worn in a holder on his belt and the tongs were carried slung over his shoulder.

The iceman was a neighborhood celebrity, on a first-name basis with the families he serviced. Always in a hurry (because of his perishable cargo), he would step lightly from the truck, walk to the back, and grab a block of ice (fifty or a hundred pounds) with his tongs. The tongs resembled a set of giant forceps, but with sharp points. He would then effortlessly sling the big block up on his shoulder and trot up the stairs.

On the back porch there was usually a metal tub where the ice waited until placed in ten- or twenty-pound chunks in the tray under the cooling compartment of the icebox. Beside the tub there was always a domestic ice pick, which all children were forbidden, under penalty of the most severe punishment, to touch.

Ice delivery was as competitive as milk sales, so service was important. Our iceman would deposit the large block, whip out his ice pick, and with the skill of long practice, split off a chunk just exactly the right size for our icebox tray. He would tap, tap, tap lightly, making a groove, then with a sharp stab, knock off just the right amount. He was an unsung artist.

The door was generally left unlocked for the iceman or he was given a key because you had to have ice. He was a trusted person. Like the milkman, he also had a reputation (deserved or not) as a Don Juan because of his intimate entry of residences.

My father had once been an iceman. Sometimes, as we were driving around town, he would point at a child and ask my mother if she thought the child resembled him. She always went for it, and I was always waiting to laugh, even though I did not understand the joke until years later.

"Why *would* he look like you?" she would ask.

"Because I used to be an *iceman*," he would say, laughing along with me and hitting the horn of his old Oldsmobile.

The iceman's arrival was a celebrated event with the impoverished clan of redheaded children down the street. Ice, to them, was a wondrous thing. When the iceman stopped there, he chipped off only a small block, just enough for cooling, but not enough for iced drinks. Even an extra ten or fifteen cents was too great a financial strain for that impoverished family.

"Iceman!" You could hear one of the redheaded boys heralding the arrival of the ice truck as if a visiting head of state or the ice cream vendor had just come to the neighborhood. They would all troop out, including Teddy, the silent two-year-old in a perpetually dirty and droopy diaper, and meet the truck a block away. Running alongside the truck, they would reach in and snatch small chunks of ice that had fallen off during previous chippings.

If the iceman was in a good mood, he would toss them a large chunk as he was leaving their house, and they would run off somewhere to divide the booty.

Ice had almost nothing to do with the story I am about to tell. In fact, had I been born a couple of years later, I would never have seen a real iceman. Frigidaire refrigerators, at that time, were already making iceboxes a thing of the past in our social stratum. Maybe only the really poor (like us) had them in 1950, at the time of this story.

Whatever the case, it was the first and last icebox in my memory. My Grandmother Goin never did learn to use the word *refrigerator.* She called all her refrigerators "iceboxes" or "Frigidaires" until she died. Even if it was a General Electric or other brand, she would say, "Get me some cream from the Frigidaire."

"It's plastic," my father said. "It's like rubber, but harder. It won't rust like metal or rot like rubber."

"It won't hurt him if he chews on it?" my mother, always the pessimist, asked.

"Why would he chew on it?" my father snapped. He was an optimist at heart. Besides, my toys were the toys he never had in his squalid childhood. "He's *three years old* now."

"I know," my mother said, "but the new baby will be along soon—and you never know with these new things."

In the middle of the polished wooden floor, I sat playing with the object under discussion. It was a red and white plastic fire engine, with rubber wheels and a friction motor that sounded a siren as it was pushed across the floor.

The fire truck was a wonder to behold. It had a tank for water and a rubber hose that unrolled. Water could be pumped through the hose by a button on top. I had never seen anything like it. All my other cars were of metal or rubber. Plastic was only then coming into common usage.

It must have been a very expensive toy. In that day the Golden Books for children could be bought for a quarter, a Popsicle cost two cents from the pushcart, and the price of some new cars was measured in hundreds of dollars.

The redheaded barbarians down the street were even impressed, and it took a lot to impress them. They would hang over the fence and watch me rev up the engine by rubbing the tires on the concrete walk, then watch as it roared away, sounding like a genuine fire engine.

It was a marvelous toy that brought me much satisfaction. The iceman was indirectly involved when I destroyed it.

"I'll need an extra block of ice today," my mother said, as the iceman dropped his load into the metal tub. Apparently we were having company and the extra ice was needed for drinks.

"All right," he said. Then, looking down at me, he asked, "What've you got there, partner?"

"It's a fire truck that really pumps water and has a siren that sounds just like a *real* siren."

"Yep," he squatted down, "sure does look like a real fire truck. What's it made of, I wonder?"

"Plastic," I replied. "It won't rust like metal or rot like rubber."

His eyebrows went up. "How old are you, son?"

"Three and I'll have a baby brother or sister soon."

"You talk a blue streak for a little 'un," he said.

"My aunts and uncles say I'm a *jeenyus*," I modestly replied.

"Maybe you are," he said. "You need to make sure you keep this here truck away from heat. Just about the only way you can hurt plastic is with heat. Or so I've read."

He went to get the second block of ice, having planted a seed. I watched him thoughtfully, then went back to fighting imaginary fires. It was later that day when the phone rang, causing my mother to leave the oven open as she was preparing to bake something.

I hurtled by her in the hallway, playing famous racecar driver in my blue, pedal-powered car as she went to answer the telephone. Screeching to a halt on the flowered linoleum, I noticed two things: my red plastic fire engine, which I had left in the kitchen, and the oven door standing open. My mother almost never did that.

In fact, she lived in terror of fire and things electrical. I remember a newspaper clipping taped to the icebox that was pointed out to me often. It was a blurred photograph of two children who had perished in a house fire.

"That's what happens to children who play with matches," Momma would often tell me. I have no idea where or even when the children, a boy and girl, both with bangs, had perished by fire, but I remember the newspaper clipping vividly.

The open oven, however, had no connection to matches. It must have seemed a prime opportunity to find out if the iceman knew what he was talking about.

Getting out of my blue racecar, I glanced down the hall and saw my mother deep in conversation. Picking up the red and white fire engine, I gingerly set it on one of the wire racks. Apparently the oven was on low heat, as I was able to do it without singeing myself.

There was sufficient heat to test the theory, however.

The red plastic soon began to wrinkle. The rubber hose

smoldered. In the course of a few minutes I watched the marvelous red and white fire engine with the friction motor turn into a charred lump.

The experiment over, I jumped back into my blue racer and roared away. It was only a few minutes until my mother, attracted by the smell of smoldering plastic, discovered the experiment.

"David!"

"What?" I asked, wheeling into the kitchen in my blue racecar.

She had the shelf pulled out and was scraping strings of molten plastic from it.

"Did you put your fire engine in the oven?"

I knew the question was more than rhetorical, though we were alone in the house. It was obvious that one of us had done it. I merely nodded yes.

"Why in the world would you do such a thing? Don't you know how expensive it was?"

I merely shrugged, having not the concepts with which to judge "expensive," as opposed to "cheap."

"You could have burned the house down! Go to your room!"

The rest of the story is lost to memory. What my father had to say about it, if anything, has escaped me. Years later, listening to my mother tell the story (while laughing) to other people, I could have cleared up the mystery of why I did it. For some reason, I never did—not until now.

It was the iceman's fault.

3

Thomas and the Easter Chick

*T*HOMAS WAS A gray and black tiger-striped alley cat. It was one of his siblings I first saw, when the little girl next door came home with it.

"Mr. Barrett gave it to me," she said, "for free." She lifted the kitten for me to look at, filling my young soul with envy. I charged into the house and found my mother going about her kitchen duties.

"Momma, Mr. Barrett gave Susan a kitten for free. Can I have one?"

"You already have a dog and a rabbit," she said reasonably, "and the pigeon is yours too."

"But I don't have a cat."

"Maybe Susan will let you play with her kitten."

"It's not the same. I want a kitten of my own."

"We'll see," my mother said.

"The only one we have left," Mrs. Barrett said, staring sadly through her thick glasses, "is this sickly little one."

"I want it!" I began to dance around. "I want it, Momma."

"But it's sick. Look at its little eyes. They're matted shut," my mother said dubiously, studying the tiny gray and black bundle of fur.

"He'll get better. I know he will. Can I have him? *Please!*"

Momma, of course, relented and we went home with the sickly kitten. As I watched her clean its eyes, a love affair began. I cannot remember the name of the black cocker spaniel, the pigeon, or the white rabbit that shared the back yard with me, but I will never forget Thomas the tomcat.

From that day forward, Thomas thrived. While he was small enough, I carried him everywhere I went. Thomas had to be put outside when I took a nap. Otherwise he would climb into the bed and lightly bat at my ears until I woke up to play with him.

In a few months, he was too big for me to carry in my arms. Instead, I walked around with my arm around his neck. Thomas would walk along behind me, half-walking, half-dragged, unprotesting. People would stop to stare.

"I've never seen such a patient cat," a neighbor said, "especially a tomcat. It acts like it really loves the child, but, of course, cats don't have feelings for anyone."

I knew better, though. In my three-and-a-half-year-old heart, I knew Thomas loved me. Oh, he roamed at night, just like all tomcats. When I was awake, though, he was there in the back yard with me. He would lie, licking his paws, sometimes watching the tame pigeon fly around on the back porch. Unknown to me, he was contemplating a future meal.

That Thomas was a beast of prey had ceased to be a secret to me early in our relationship. I never held it against him when he finally ate the pigeon. I knew it was his job as a cat to catch and eat game. I had first seen him in action early one morning in the kitchen when no one else was awake in the house.

A mouse had apparently decided to work overtime that morning. It was still in the garbage container when I let Thomas into the house. The furry gray rodent made a dash across the kitchen, but was stopped dead in its tracks as

Thomas landed on it with both front feet. The mouse squeaked once, then was quiet.

An older child might have been frightened or disgusted. At three, I was fascinated.

Most people have heard of "cat and mouse games." I watched my first one that morning. The mouse, unhurt, stared out from under the cat's paw with glittering black eyes. Slowly Thomas lifted his paw. The mouse shot out, only to be caught by the lightning-fast slap of the other paw.

On my hands and knees, I watched the life and death drama played out. With a casual air, Thomas began to bat the mouse back and forth between his paws. For a while, the mouse attempted to escape. Finally, after many futile attempts at escape, it sat in resignation.

When the mouse became still, Thomas reached down between his paws and bit into the creature's neck with a crunching sound. I sat quietly as he ate the mouse in small meticulous bites, until only the tail was left. He consumed it slowly, like a piece of spaghetti, licked the drops of blood from the floor, then cleaned his paws.

His meal and bath over, he stretched and looked at me, as if to say, "What's on the agenda today?"

It bothered me not in the least that my closest companion in the world was a killer. Small children have no preconceived notions of morality.

"Wake up and see what we have, David," my mother said.

I opened my eyes and gave a squeal of delight. Boldly stalking about and pecking at the bedspread was a chick. It was the same color of blue as one of the eggs in my Easter basket, carefully stored in the refrigerator from the day before.

I have not seen colored Easter chicks in years. The animal rights activists have stopped the practice. In those days, however, colored chicks and ducklings were a standard feature of Easter. You would see them everywhere the week before the holiday, bustling about in multicolored hues, in store windows and on the streets.

"Is it mine?" I asked, as if it could have belonged to any-one else.

"It sure is," my father said.

At that moment, the chick made a large and disgusting stain on my bedspread as it absent-mindedly walked about. No chicken, adult or baby, has ever had the brains to be housebroken. I imagine that is why they have never become popular pets with urban dwellers. My mother quickly snatched it up and put it into a cardboard box. In a moment she was wiping the bedspread with a damp rag.

"Let's eat breakfast," Momma said, "then we'll dress up and take pictures in our Easter clothes."

At the table I had my standard breakfast, watching the blue chick skitter about in the cardboard box. My standard breakfast was an egg over medium, two pieces of toast (pre-buttered and cooked in the oven) and hot chocolate. It took triple bypass coronary surgery to modify that wonderfully delicious high cholesterol diet—and I still cheat sometimes.

Normally I would have been playing with Thomas by that time, but the chick had taken my mind off everything else. The cat was not on my mind at all as Momma dressed me in my new Easter clothes and combed my hair, attempting to subdue the cowlick on the back of my head.

Outside in the bright early morning sun, my mother snapped and rolled the black and white film in the box cam-era as I mugged away, happy to be the center of attention.

"Put the chicken down," she said, "and look at me."

"No!" I heard my father cry helplessly as I deposited the chick on the ground.

Thomas had been lurking under the steps. As the chicken touched ground, he darted out and snapped it up. Before anyone could move, the gray and black tiger tom was under the porch and out of reach.

"My chicken!" I screamed. "I want my chicken!" I col-lapsed on the ground, screaming and kicking, perfectly aware of the chick's intended fate.

"We'll get you another chick," Momma said, trying to comfort me.

"I want *that* chick. Make Thomas bring it back!" I screamed with all the terror and rage of a three-year-old.

"Cats are not like dogs," Daddy began, "you can't expect a cat to—"

At that moment, Thomas emerged from under the house and ran to me. He dropped the blue chick at my feet, looked up at me, then dashed back under the porch.

"I don't believe that just happened," my mother said, the evidence before her eyes.

Scooping the chick up in his hands, my father rushed into the house and ran cold water over it. It revived and in a moment was walking around again, unconcerned. Chickens also have short memories.

"Cats don't have feelin's," my father said in a puzzled voice, "but it *looked* like he knew exactly what he was doin'."

"I know," my mother said, "he brought it back and dropped it right in front of David."

"I wonder why he didn't kill it as soon as he picked it up?" my father wondered aloud.

The answer to that question, I already knew. Cats play with their prey before they kill.

For the rest of the day and for years to come, my parents told the story of the Easter chick. Everyone puzzled over it, because it is a well-known fact that cats are self-centered, unfeeling creatures.

At the age of three, though, I knew perfectly well why Thomas had brought the chick back to me when I cried. The intervening years and experiences with other cats have not changed my opinion.

Thomas the tomcat loved me. There was no other logical explanation.

I don't remember what happened to the chicken.

—4—

Work Was Made for Fools and Mules

MY FATHER HATED all things military. It was a personal grudge, having to do with human dignity. He was never eloquent enough to verbalize such a concept, however, beyond saying: "They treat you like a dog, not a man. *Nobody* should be treated the way a soldier is treated."

As a World War II marine, he had done his part. Every detail of his military career had to be dug out, though. It was not something he liked to discuss. Dad was dead for years before Mom told me about how he had found his best friend, sitting in an outdoor privy, throat slashed in a final act of despair—the day before the war ended.

Twenty years after leaving Iwo Jima, the slightest noise in the night would bring him out of the bed in a fighting stance, drenched in sweat, eyes wide in terror. He only spoke of those days if pushed, and then only briefly. He would speak of night patrols and standing guard in the black, humid jungles of Pacific islands.

My father was of the opinion that the military broke the human spirit, then became a haven for broken men.

★   ★   ★

My uncle Hobert, fifteen years older than my father, was drafted into the army at the outbreak of World War II. He became a professional soldier—except for short breaks—and stayed for over twenty years, mostly as an artilleryman.

"He was a good man," Dad would say, "until the army ruined him—a good worker." Being a good worker to my father was a religious tenet.

Uncle Hobe, however, did not share my father's belief in the sacred dignity of labor, nor my father's belief in temperance. Hobe apparently got drunk in the early days of the war and remained that way for the rest of his life, with only sporadic periods of sobriety.

Unlike my father, Hobe was more than glad to discuss things military. I do not know if it was the difference between infantryman and artilleryman, or just a difference between men.

His brief visits were a time of celebration for me. There were always a new garrison cap and patches and ribbons for me to wear when he came. He taught me drill and ceremony when I was barely walking.

"Hup, two, three!" he would intone, sitting in a chair, beer in hand, as I marched up and down the walk, carrying a toy rifle and wearing an oversized military cap.

In all but one picture I ever saw of my Uncle Hobert while he was in the military, he had a beer or whiskey in his hand, glassy eyes, and an obvious flush on his face, no matter what country he happened to be in.

His visits always left me playing soldier for weeks afterward, stalking my pets from ambush and sniping at passing cars. It was a shock when he came home in my fourth year of life and said he had "quit the army."

"You'll go back," my father said, "you always do."

"Nope. I'm finished with it. It's time to get on with my life." He was angry about a recent court-martial. I would later find that he was court-martialed thirteen times during his first eight years of service—before he finally cleaned up his act. Such behavior would not be tolerated today, but then apparently it was common.

"I've heard that before," my father said, drinking one of his rare beers, which he gave up altogether when he became a Baptist at twenty-six.

"No. I mean it! I want a good *civilian* job. You're the foreman over at Tucker's, aren't you?"

"Yeah, but we're a small outfit. Everybody has to pull his weight."

"I can pull my weight," Hobe said indignantly. "You used to work with me."

"Yeah, but that was before the army ruined you. You're too lazy now." Daddy was never noted for his reticence of opinion.

"By God! I mean it. I'm turnin' my life around." Hobert banged his fist on the table. He was a short man, even shorter than his brother's five and a half feet, with the same swarthy complexion, though not as muscular.

"All right," my father sighed, "do you have money for work clothes?"

"No, but if you'll loan it to me, I'll give it back payday." He took a big swig of beer and wiped his mouth with the back of his hand, eyes glassed and face flushed.

"How did it go?" Momma asked, as Hobe and my father sat down for supper, the evening meal. There was corn on the cob, fried potatoes, fresh tomatoes, and beans for protein. Meat was not an everyday staple.

"Rough," Uncle Hobe said, spearing an ear of corn, "but a lot better than servin' in an army that don't appreciate my better qualities."

"What kind of work are you doin'?" Momma asked, trying to stimulate conversation.

"He's a painter," Daddy replied, "but he'll work up to fabrication as time passes. It's rough, but only temporary."

"You're *right*, it's rough," Hobert said. "I've been sprayin' that same orange paint all day. You can *taste* it, even through the mask!"

"You're just out of practice," my father said.

"Will you march me around after supper?" I asked.

"Not tonight," he said, getting up from the table. "I'm gonna walk down to the store and get a beer."

"Remember, we have to be up at five," Daddy said.

"I know!" Uncle Hobe answered, just a little too sharply as he was leaving. My mother looked at my father meaningfully, before he could respond.

"He's not here," Daddy said, slamming the bedroom door. "He didn't come home last night—and he knows we've got a big job to get out this week."

"Maybe he had a good reason," Momma said.

"The same reason as always. He's drunk somewhere in Lonsdale at some whore's place. He got paid yesterday and he won't have a dime today."

"Give him one chance, anyway. He's tried hard the last three weeks."

"I'll think about it while I'm doin' his job and mine today," my father said, stalking out of the house.

Uncle Hobert had managed to last three weeks. Each morning, he left carrying a lunch identical to the one my mother had packed for my father. Each night he came home more morose, covered with orange primer paint. The night before he had gone out "for a beer" and had not returned.

It was noon when I looked up from a solitary game of marbles to see him staggering through the gate.

"Hey, solsier," he yelled, "whers' yer weapon."

"Put up," I answered. "Playin' soldier's not much fun by yourself."

He fell several times getting up the steps. I followed him in as he staggered past my mother, mumbling something as he went. In a few minutes, he was lost in fitful, tormented sleep, banging the walls and moaning, as he always did when drunk.

"Why does he do that?" I asked, climbing up on a stool.

"I don't know," Momma answered as she put a fresh diaper on my brother, Larry, who was a few months old then, but of little interest to me. He could not talk or walk, took up my mother's time, and had gotten me in trouble when I fed him sunflower seeds one evening. My parents had found him almost choked, after I stuffed his mouth with the edible seeds. There was no malice involved; I was merely sharing as I had been taught.

"Daddy's gonna be mad, huh?"

"He's *already* mad. I'm gonna try and get him to wait until in the mornin' before he says anything, though."

My father was extraordinarily calm, frighteningly calm. Aside from asking if Hobert had gotten home, he did not mention him during supper. My father's calm was always more scary than his yelling.

The eruption didn't come until morning.

"Get up," my father said in an even voice. "I covered for you yesterday, but we're behind. Let's get movin'."

Uncle Hobe sat up in the bed, apparently still a little drunk. "I can't go in. I'm sick."

"You're not sick; you're hung over. Now, get up and drink some coffee. You're goin' to work today. I gave my word that you'd be dependable." My father turned to walk away, the matter settled, as far as he was concerned.

"I didn't give my word," Hobert mumbled belligerently.

"Yes you did. You gave your word to me, and you know how I feel about that."

"Well, then let me tell you how I feel." Hobert spoke in a sing-song voice. "*Work was made for fools and mules—and I ain't neither one.*"

My father was across the room in three paces. He jerked Hobert from the bed by his T-shirt collar. I watched from the hall, fascinated, unaware before that moment that adults had physical conflicts.

"Bill!" my mother screamed as my father's fist went back. "Don't hit your *brother!*"

Daddy stopped, lowered his fist, then pushed Uncle Hobe back on the bed.

"Get your stuff out of here. Be gone when I get back. You're worthless, except for soldierin'."

Neither my mother nor Hobert attempted to argue with that.

After several cups of coffee, Uncle Hobe packed his duffel bag. Momma gave him a couple of dollars for cab fare and he left.

When next we heard from him a year or so later, he was stationed in Texas. A year after that, he came for a visit, as if nothing had happened. He never left the army again until retirement.

From the incident that morning, I learned that adults were as different from each other as children. I learned how my father valued his work and how he hated the lifestyle from which he had come.

Later, when I became a soldier briefly, the drill instructor said that I was as good at drill and ceremony as anyone he had ever trained.

— 5 —

Trailer Trash
from Tennessee

WHEN I WAS FOUR and my brother a
toddler, we went to Aiken, South Carolina. My father, an
ironworker, had hired on to help build the nearby plant,
which construction families simply called "the H-Bomb
Plant." I don't know what was eventually manufactured
there, but that's what we called it.

It was a great adventure for me. I was fascinated by the
flat country, all pines and sand, quite a change from the
rolling green hills and mountains of East Tennessee. I had
absolutely no idea of our poverty.

The trailer in which we lived was about eighteen feet long,
but things are usually remembered as having been bigger
when seen from a child's point of view. A tiny bedroom was
at one end, which my then-pregnant mother shared with my
father. At the other end was a couch bed on which my
brother and I slept. In the middle was a refrigerator, a gas
stove, a sink that was big enough for washing dishes, and a
table that folded against the wall when not in use.

There was no bathroom in the trailer. A block away was a
communal bathroom, showers, and a laundry room. The

37

place called Roman's Trailer Park was a melting pot of people from many different places, drawn by high construction wages. To me, it was wonderful to have a distant bathroom and shower, providing a chance for high adventure.

The first morning I was there, a wonderful thing happened: a house went by.

We were at the very front of the park, with an unobstructed view of the highway. I had never seen anything like it. Moving a house is not unheard of, but it is a rare occurrence in East Tennessee because of the rugged terrain, all up and down, ridges and hollows. A quarter mile of flat road is considered a long stretch.

I watched in awe as the house was towed by, followed by yapping mongrel dogs, certain that they alone were causing the house to flee down the road.

A fantasy seized me. Suddenly the world was moving under my feet. Eventually the Wild West would pass me if I waited long enough. The entire world would come by and I would hop on at a place of choice, preferably a place with cowboys and Indians.

As the house passed out of sight, I became aware of the children across the street in front of a shack on stilts. I had never seen such a pathetic house, even in the poorest of Knoxville neighborhoods. It was gray and faded and had no paint whatsoever. In the back was a precariously leaning outdoor toilet.

"Trailer trash, trailer trash, go back home," they chanted.

Having no idea what they were talking about at first, I thought they were trying to be friendly. The tone quickly told me otherwise. Suddenly one of them hurled a rock toward me. I retaliated. It was my first encounter with prejudice, but children the world over understand rock fights.

"At least *my* home has paint on it," I yelled at them.

The distance was too great for us to hit each other, but the rock fight continued until my attention was caught by the wailing of a child.

Discontinuing hostilities, I wandered to the end of our trailer and saw a woman leading what appeared to be a little

girl of about my age by the hand. Later I would discover that
it was a little boy, whose mother (unaware of modern child
psychology) put a dress on him and paraded him through
the park every time he wet the bed.

"Whatcha doin'?" I asked.

"Just messin' around." It was the little boy whose mother
had dragged him through the park wearing a dress a couple
of days before. He had reddish brown hair and a lot of freckles. That day he was dressed as I was, in a T-shirt, shorts, and
canvas sneakers. He was carrying a rifle.

"What kinda gun is that?" I asked. It was a marvelous gun.
That much I already knew, just like the ones I had seen in
the movies.

"It's a Red Ryder gun," he said. "I got the only one in this
trailer park."

"Does it shoot BBs?" I asked.

"Nope. Even better than that."

"What?" How anything could be better than a BB gun was
beyond my comprehension.

"Watch." He stuck the open end of the rifle into the wet
sand, pulled the lever to cock it, and pointed it into the air.
Pow! It sounded like a real gun going off. Sand spewed out,
raining down everywhere.

"Can I shoot it?"

"Yeah, I guess." He handed it to me and I began to slay
imaginary monsters.

"What's yer name?" he asked.

"David. What's yours?"

"Frankie. Where're you from?"

"Tennessee."

"Me too. Most here ain't, though. Most of 'em is Yankees, my
mama says. There's a real Indian lives here too, but no niggers."

"What's a nigger?" I was not familiar with the term.

"You know, jungle-bunnies, colored people."

"OK. I know whatcha mean now." I had seen black people, though I had never met one and would not for years to
come.

"I bet you ain't got the nerve to shoot me in the eye," Frankie said, leaning forward. He pulled his lower eyelid down, exposing the pink and red veins against the white eyeball.

To this day, I have no idea what was in Frankie's mind— or mine either, for that matter.

"I bet I *do.*"

"Bet ya *don't!* Go ahead if you got the nerve." He leaned toward me again. "Double dog dare ya!"

Raising the rifle, I took aim and pulled the trigger, point blank. Frankie's eye disappeared, covered by a glob of wet sand. My mother, who had been watching, ran from the trailer as Frankie let out a blood-curdling scream and headed for home.

"Hey Frankie," I yelled, "you forgot yer gun."

"I got to do it," Frankie said, staring balefully at me through his one good and one swollen and bloodshot eye. He and another urchin had accosted me on the way to the communal bathroom. "You *hurt* me. It took all day fer my mama to get that sand out. My eye is still red."

"You *told* me to do it," I said rationally. "I only done it 'cause you told me to."

"Don't matter. My mama says you shoulda had more sense."

"I *got* more sense. It was your idea."

"Don't matter," said the other boy, a pudgy child of five with a clipped Yankee accent. "You hurt Frankie and we're gonna whip you for doin' it." He was grinning with an evil leer, obviously looking forward to it. Clenched in his fist was a broomstick.

"Y'all had better leave me alone," I bluffed, trying to walk by. It was my very first experience with violence.

A moment later they were pounding me. The shock of being physically assaulted for the first time was unreal. When the broomstick connected with my mouth, I broke loose and ran home screaming, the coppery taste of blood in my mouth.

I was met at the door by my parents. My father stood in his dirty work clothes, newspaper in hand, as my mother washed the blood from my mouth. When she had finished, he pulled my lip down to look at the small cut.

Weeping in pain and righteous indignation, with the taste of dirty pennies still strong in my mouth, I waited for soothing words.

"Stop cryin', now!" Daddy said. "It's only a little cut."

The sobbing halted.

"Do you know who did this?"

I nodded affirmatively.

"Were they your age or bigger?"

"There was two, 'bout my age," I said.

"Then get out there and whip both of them. Do it now. Sometimes you lose. It can't be helped. It's all right to come home bloody, but if you ever again come in from a fight cryin', I'll whip you again when you get here. Understand?"

"Bill, he's just a little boy—" my mother began.

"This is *his* fight. If they run him home now, they'll do it every day. It's a *rough* world." He turned to me again. "Go on. Do it!"

Years later a psychologist would express horror that a parent would say such a thing to a small child. My father was right, though. The pain of a beating is momentary; the pain of living in fear goes on and on.

The two boys were near the communal bathhouse, no doubt giggling about what they had done to me, when I swooped down on them, less afraid of them than of my father's wrath. They had no idea that they were about to be thrashed by Prince Valiant of the Sunday color comics, sent on a quest by his father, the fierce warrior king.

The fat boy with the broomstick, shock in his eyes, tried to rise and hit me with it as I ran at them screaming like a maniac, but I wrested it from him and began to flail both of them with it.

Moments later, I watched in triumph as they ran screaming home. The memory is as vivid now as it was that day.

I climbed the mountain of red earth, surveying the children standing at the top. There were six of them, five boys and a girl, all near my age. You could see the entire world when you stood on top.

Actually, it was a mound of dirt from a freshly dug cesspool, about eight feet high.

"What'er y'all doin'?" I asked. Like me, the boys were dressed in shorts and sneakers. The little girl was wearing only cotton panties and sandals.

"We're diggin' a lake," a boy with a runny nose said. "When it's done, we're gonna drown a toad in it." There was no toad in sight, but I took his word.

"Can I play?"

"Do you live in this trailer park?" he asked suspiciously. We had learned to close ranks against the native South Carolinians, who called us "trailer trash."

"Yeah. I live in the green trailer at the very front."

"All right," he wiped his nose with the back of his hand, "but I'm the boss."

With our bare hands we dug in the fresh red earth until the boy with the runny nose proclaimed it deep enough— about six inches by eight inches.

"Now we need water," the foreman said. It was a problem, indeed. There could be no toad drowning without water. We had water in our trailers, but we couldn't let our mothers know what we were doing because we had all been told to stay away from freshly dug cesspool holes. A child had spent the night in one of them a few weeks before, becoming the focus of an all-night hunt.

Without further ado, a redheaded boy with brilliant orange freckles opened his fly and began to urinate into the six-inch-deep, dry lake bed. A moment later, the rest of the boys had joined in. As we stepped back, pleased with our handiwork, the little girl stepped out of her panties and squatted over the lake to add her contribution to the engineering feat.

Catching my breath, I immediately dropped down on all fours for an unembarrassed look. Never until that moment had I known there was a difference, except for clothes, between little boys and little girls.

"Whatsa matter?" the little girl asked. "Aintcha never seen a girl *down there* before?" She spoke in a grating northern dialect.

I admitted that I had not and continued to stare, fascinated. Finishing her part of the lake she stood up, and seeing that she was the absolute center of attention, dimpled up in a smile.

"Here. Youse guys can look at it close if you want." She leaned backward slightly, using her hands to spread the display for plain viewing. We all leaned in for a closer look with bated breath.

"Deborah!" An indignant female voice yelled. The little girl scrambled for her panties as we all turned, terror-stricken, to see a young woman with a red face staring at us in outrage. That it was the little girl's mother, none of us had any doubt.

We all stampeded away from the scene of the crime. As I rounded the corner of my trailer, I heard the first smack land on the five-year-old Lolita's bare behind. Crawling up under the trailer, my favorite hiding place, I waited an hour or so for the outraged mother to arrive and snitch me out for my part in the incident.

She never came, though. The fear and terror faded. Finally I crawled out and began to ride my bicycle around the front yard, becoming a daredevil on a big red motorcycle, occasionally thinking of the little girl and what I had seen.

I had discovered a great mystery.

— 6 —

You Must Be Born Again

M Y FATHER, William Henry "Bill" Hunter, raised a Roman Catholic, often said that he had become a Christian in 1952 at the age of twenty-six.

"I had a form of godliness," he would testify of his Roman Catholic upbringing, "that was taking me straight to hell. The Bible told me, and I'll tell you, *you must be born again.*"

My father saw the universe in terms of good and evil, right and wrong, black and white. There was no middle ground. You walked the straight and narrow or you fell into the pit. He saw leisure time as one of the devil's most efficient tools and made certain that neither he nor those around him ever had much leisure time.

Bill Hunter had never read history, except the Bible. He could not have told you who Martin Luther was. If it could not be found between the covers of the Bible, or if you had not lived it, then, by his standards, a thing was just not worth knowing.

Despite his lack of knowledge about Martin Luther, my father had something in common with him: at a point in their lives, both began to question certain tenets of Roman

Catholicism, particularly the part about being born into the Church.

It was the practice of granting papal "indulgences" as a fundraiser that set Martin Luther on his path; for my father, I believe, it was the sense of being an outsider.

Bill Hunter had never belonged anywhere and had rejected his inheritance, such as it was. His mother was a nominal Roman Catholic who made her children attend parochial school until they were old enough to rebel. They attended by charity, being among the poorest of the poor.

As a grown man he still burned with the shame of going to school in rags, among children whose parents could afford to dress them well and send them to the expensive private school. He was there, but he never belonged. Furthermore, while going to Catholic schools, he lived among predominantly Protestant people, who often teased him about his religion.

His sense of isolation was not helped by belonging to a family that was known far and wide as white trash. Raised by a drunken brawler and a bitter woman, the older children, for the most part, partook of the heritage.

The last time he saw his father, my grandfather, alive was at the age of twelve. William Franklin Hunter had come for a visit with his children at Christmas. He kissed his youngest son good-bye as he left.

When his father was out of sight, young Bill Hunter's mother washed his mouth with gasoline. His father, she truthfully told him, had a terrible social disease. It was syphilis. Eventually he died from it, alone, at the county poor house at the age of forty-one. My father never escaped *that* stigma either.

Salvation by inheritance and birth, anything that came by inheritance, Bill Hunter rejected, though he could not have verbalized that concept. He began to look around for enlightenment.

It was an ordinary day for me in my fifth year, when my father came to grips with God.

★   ★   ★

"You kids get ready. We're goin' over to your Mam-maw's," my mother said. She always said "to your Mam-maw's," though my grandfather lived there too.

Trips to our grandparents' house were regular events. For all practical purposes, we only had one set of grandparents. Grandmother Hunter, poor as a church mouse until in her forties, had inherited Kansas oil money and promptly moved to Saint Petersburg, Florida, where she eventually married her third husband, a prosperous Ohio farmer.

To me, at the age of five, Grandmother Hunter was a shadowy figure, who popped up once in a while for a visit, usually staying only long enough to dye her hair.

She did not marry the Ohio farmer until I was six. He managed to tolerate her for several years before trying to abandon her—but that's another story.

Larry and I charged out to our new Studebaker that evening, unaware that our world was about to change. It was the only new car our father ever bought, and it was a beauty: pale green and cream colored, from which emanated the rich, unforgettable smell of new leather.

At five, I was enthralled with the idea of spaceships and ray guns. Every time we got into the car, Larry and I were strapping in for a mission somewhere across the solar system.

"Ready!" I yelled, as our father fired up the powerful V-8 Studebaker. "Blastoff!"

Momma sat holding our little sister in her lap, as Daddy concentrated on the driving. Usually he was talking, waving his arms, his ruddy complexion becoming even darker as it flushed with excitement.

That day, however, he had nothing to say. Looking back, I am certain that his inner conflict had been going on for a while. The subtle nature of his turmoil was beyond my understanding, though I do remember one thing from that period.

We recently had moved from South Carolina to a small house on Paris Road in Knoxville. I remember no work projects at that time in Daddy's life. He sat around a lot, which was a very unusual thing. Most of his life was spent building something or changing something he had built. A few hours before his death he was still tinkering, still working. I have no idea how long he was in turmoil before the crisis.

"Enemy ahead! Man the guns," I yelled.

"Ready!" Larry piped out.

I remember exactly where we were. Daddy had just driven through the railroad tunnel at Central Avenue and Heiskell Street. Without warning, he wheeled off to the side of Heiskell, killed the engine, put his face on the steering wheel, and began to weep—great chest-wrenching sobs.

The spaceship ground to a halt. I sat stunned, uncomprehending. I cried, my mother cried, my grandmother cried. Even space heroes cried under pressure, but my father had never cried until then. It had not occurred to me that such a thing was possible.

"I can't stand it anymore," he wept, pounding on the steering wheel with his fists, "I surrender."

Momma was as stunned as I was. Whether she had seen him cry before, I do not know. I doubt it. She started to touch him but withdrew her hand.

It was obvious that everything had ceased to exist for my father at that moment, except for the God with whom he was conversing. Though that concept was beyond my understanding, I knew that some great and earth-shattering thing had happened.

When he had recovered, he started the car and drove on to my grandparents' house, his face still wet with tears.

"I gotta go talk to somebody," Daddy said, letting us out of the car. "I'll be back in a while."

Later I would find that he went to a friend's house. The friend was a Southern Baptist, who took him to see his pastor. That was how we came to be Southern Baptists.

"I was saved at the wheel of my car," he would testify for the rest of his life. "I met the Lord in the free pardon of sin, driving down the street in my automobile. I came to understand that very day, that you *must* be born again."

Bill Hunter never faltered, never looked back. At last, he *belonged* somewhere. The next Sunday my brother and I were in Sunday school at Third Creek Baptist Church, where my father's friend was a member, wearing new clothes purchased for the occasion. It was rare after that if we missed Sunday school. Eventually my father was ordained a deacon, a job that he took very seriously.

Never after that day on Heiskell Street did he break covenant with his God. There was never again an alcoholic beverage in the house (that being Southern Baptist doctrine). The times that he lapsed and uttered even a slang word, I can count on the fingers of one hand. Among hard-drinking, women-chasing ironworkers, he became a legend as the man who did none of these things.

There is a photograph of my father that is emblazoned in my memory. He is standing waist deep in a creek, wearing a white shirt for the occasion. His head is back, his face is looking to the heavens. He was never an articulate man, but that expression was his epic poem.

Even now, as I write these words, tears are running freely down my face. In the picture, the preacher is about to baptize my father by immersion. The expression on his dark, ruddy face will always stand as a testimony in my mind. His expression was joyous, one of the few times I ever saw him in his brief life without lines of worry.

"I don't *think* I'm going to heaven; I don't *guess* I'm going to heaven; I don't *wish* to go to heaven; I *know* I'm going to heaven—because I know Jesus in the free pardon of sin."

This speech was delivered, with his fist pounding the table top, to my Roman Catholic grandmother during a theological discussion after supper one night.

If I am ever asked to name the events that changed my life, that set me down the paths I have followed, I will have to name that day on Heiskell Street when I saw my father weep.

He taught me that human lives can turn around; that we are not helpless pawns; that salvation, however we define it, is within our grasp.

I understood later what I did not understand as a child. It is true that, to forge ahead, we must sometimes shed the old and leave it behind.

Anything—even a new birth—is possible to those who believe.

7

The Night I Met the Devil

*I*T'LL BE HALLOWEEN next week," Tim, the first grader from next door, said. "We'll put on our costooms and go out collectin' candy—tons and tons of it."

"Oh yeah?" I was five then, and we were still living in the small house on Paris Road where we had moved after returning from South Carolina.

Tim, a chunky boy of six, was already in school, while I would not go for another year. Since he was an older and more experienced man, I listened avidly to what he had to say.

"Last year I was a ghost. This year I'm gonna be a pirate, with a sword (he pronounced *sword* the way it is spelled) and a black patch over my eye. I'll skeer the little kids to death."

I listened, fascinated. It was the first Halloween I remember. Apparently, it had made no impression on me previously. That year, however, I was definitely on fire to celebrate it, inspired by Tim's tales of terror.

"You knock on a door and when they answer, you yell, 'Trick or treat.' That means they gotta give you candy, or you trick 'em."

"What kinda trick?" I asked, entranced.

"I dunno. They've always give me candy," Tim answered.

"A mean trick, I bet."

"Yeah. What'er you gonna be?" he asked, changing the subject.

"It's a secret," I lied, ashamed to admit that the subject had not even come up at my house.

"You don't even know," he said perceptively.

"Yeah, I know. It'll be better than any ol' pirate. I can tell ya *that*. I gotta get home for supper."

There were, I knew, things to discuss with my mother. Charging into the kitchen, I took off my jacket and sat down at the table. Momma was frying potatoes, pinto beans simmered on the stove, and there was cornbread in the oven. It was our staple diet.

"Tim says it'll be Halloween next week."

"That's right," she answered, turning the sizzling potatoes.

"What am I gonna be?"

"I really hadn't thought about it. Larry's still too little to go out and there's nobody to keep your baby sister. Your daddy has Bible study next week."

"I *gotta* go. Ever'body's gonna be out."

"Don't get excited. I'll check with Katie and see if you can go with Herman."

"When?"

"When I get time."

"Will it be today?"

"Yes, but we still have to ask your Daddy."

I went to my room and terrorized my brother with stories of monsters, ghosts, and pirates, killing the eternity before I would really know anything.

He was, I pleasantly discovered, terrified by my stories.

"Katie says she'll take David out with Herman for Halloween next week," Momma said over supper.

I glanced up, surprised. Somehow I had missed the telephone call she made to Katie. Daddy took a bite of beans and looked at me and then at my brother.

"I'm not sure how I feel about celebratin' a heathen holiday." He paused and poured sweet pickle juice on his beans and cornbread. "It don't sound very Christian."

My heart sank. Up to that point, except for going to church every Sunday morning, the Southern Baptist Church had not affected my lifestyle. If it was going to start causing me problems, I would have to take another look at it.

"It's just a kids' holiday," Momma said. "Nobody even remembers that it's a heathen holiday. The kids just have fun."

"All right." He apparently was not set in his belief at that point, or he would never have changed his mind.

"He'll need a mask," she added.

"I wanna mast too," Larry, two and a half, piped in.

"I wanna be a spaceman," I decided on the spur of the moment.

"We'll see," our father replied. I knew how the world worked well enough to understand that he would see what was on sale Halloween eve. He never paid full price when a bargain was available.

Daddy was carrying a paper bag when he came home on that long-awaited evening. I raced across the yard as he exited the green Studebaker. It was not a grocery bag, so it had to be my mask.

Following him into the house, I watched him put the bag on top of the refrigerator—out of my grasp. To my chagrin, he went into the living groom, picked up his newspaper, and began to read.

It was an eternity before supper was served and eaten. Then he left the table and headed for the bedroom, as if nothing out of the ordinary was transpiring. It was time for Plan B. I nudged Larry and he acted right on cue, just as I had trained him.

"Daddy, did you get the masts?" he asked, toddling along behind him.

"Oh yeah," he grinned wickedly. "I almost forgot."

Bouncing along behind him, jumping from one foot to another, I knew the suspense was not over yet. Daddy peered into the bag, as if seeing it for the first time.

"Would you rather be a tiger or a black panther?" he asked Larry.

"What's a panther?" Larry inquired.

"It's a ugly ol' black cat. You'd rather be a big tiger," I said desperately, seized with visions of a sleek, black cat.

"A tiger," Larry said, being a trusting child, "I wanna be a tiger."

Daddy promptly handed Larry a yellow striped tiger mask made of lacquered fiber. To me he gave a mask with a panther's face. It was black with yellow trim. Slowly I examined it with trembling hands.

Larry pulled his mask on, turned and ran, growling, to the living room. He ran full speed into a wooden cabinet, bouncing back to the floor. At that age Larry frequently ran into things; he could trip over a shadow.

As Larry was being fussed over, I slipped out of the house and proceeded to the swing, where I found Tim playing. He looked up.

"Is that your Halloween costume?"

"Yep."

"Just a mask? I'll have a *whole* costoom," he said.

"Oh yeah. Well, my mother is sewin' the rest of my costoom. It's black and it'll have real razor blades for claws!"

"Really?" he asked, obviously impressed. "Do you wanna go with me?"

"No, I'm goin' with Herman and the rest of the *big* kids," I said haughtily. Herman was eight.

It was approximately four the next afternoon when I started nagging my mother.

"When are you takin' me over to Herman's house?"

"Not until dark. We still have to eat supper." She was changing my sister's diaper. "Now, go play."

Every five minutes or so, I was back, until finally, what seemed a lifetime later, Momma wrapped my baby sister in a blanket and put a coat on my brother.

"Let's go," she said. "I'll walk you to the front door." As we were leaving, I saw Tim come out on the front porch with his mother. His fabled pirate costume was an old felt hat with the brim folded up and a wooden sword. He did not see me, so I knew I would be able to spring my knowledge on him when he tried to brag tomorrow.

At the front door, Momma's friend Katie greeted us. "Come on in, David. Herman's still getting ready."

"How long will you be out?" my mother asked.

"Not more than a couple of hours."

"All right. I appreciate it. He wouldn't have gotten to go otherwise."

"I don't mind at all," Katie said.

"Behave yourself, David." I barely heard my mother's admonition. On the table were piles of candy. I stood looking at the multicolored wrappers, mouth watering.

Turning, I was about to say something to Katie, when I saw the apparition that had appeared in the room behind me. I froze. My tongue went numb. My breath was squeezed out of my chest by fear.

It was the devil. Not *a* devil, but *the* devil. He was just like I had heard him described once in a fire and brimstone sermon.

His feet were shiny black (painted rubber boots). His body was red (dyed long johns). In his hand was a pitchfork (genuine). His face was hideous, fangs protruding, mouth frozen into a snarl (a rubber mask).

"It's only Herman," Katie said, seeing my horrified expression. I was frozen to the floor until . . .

The devil put out his hand as if to touch me. At the same time he took a step and his long pointed tail bounced up behind him (a spring sewed into a cloth sleeve).

The springy pointed tail broke my paralysis. I hurtled down the hall toward the front door, seeking salvation. I waited for the prongs of the pitchfork to penetrate my back. I imagined the bed of hot coals Old Scratch had prepared for me. I repented every lie I had ever told, lies being the extent of my sins at the time.

The doorknob loomed ahead. I grabbed it and tried to twist, but the complexities of machinery were beyond me at that moment. Katie tried to pick me up, but I was clinging to the knob for dear life.

"It's only Herman," Katie said. "Take the mask off, Herman!" I closed my eyes as the devil bore down on me. I could hear his foul breath, hissing through the twisted mouth.

"Open your eyes," Katie said.

Finally, when the pitchfork did not rip me apart, I opened one eye. Herman's head had appeared above the devil's body. "It's only me in a costume," Herman said. "Come on, let's get some candy."

Turning loose of the doorknob, I attempted to regain my dignity. I straightened my coat.

"I *knew* it was Herman all the time," I told them.

"Of course you did," Katie said. "Let's see what kind of mask you have."

For the rest of the night, I made certain that I stayed behind Herman. I knew he was not really the devil, but it was as close as I ever wanted to get to the real thing.

We collected a lot of candy that night—and I vowed to listen closely to our pastor thereafter. It was time, I decided, to see if I was old enough to be baptized.

The devil had put the fear of God in me.

8

Faraway Glasses and a Phantom Ship

YOU CAN ACTUALLY see the Phantom Spaceship, flashing across your wall," the radio announcer said. "All you have to do is buy a box of Wheat Munchies. The Phantom Spaceship card is *free*."

Focused with all the intensity of one who has just turned six, I was listening to a radio show about my favorite spaceman hero (we will call him Captain John). His sponsor was Wheat Munchies (another pseudonym).

A real spaceship that could be seen in my own house on Brown Avenue! The very thought sent chills up and down my spine. I dashed into the living room where Momma was sewing and Daddy was reading his newspaper.

"If you buy a box of Wheat Munchies, you get a card that lets you see a *real* spaceship in your own home," I said breathlessly.

"You wouldn't eat Wheat Munchies the last time I bought them," my mother said, introducing hard reality into my fantasy. "You told me they tasted awful."

I stood for a moment, stunned, condemned out of my own mouth, before inspiration struck. "That was the *old* Wheat Munchies. Now they're new and improved!"

"They just changed the box. It's the same cereal and it'll still taste like cardboard," my father said. He was of the impression that any cereal invented after Mr. Kellogg rolled out his original corn flakes in Battle Creek, Michigan, was a cheap rip-off, not worthy to be called breakfast cereal.

"Nope. Eddie tried it, and he says it's all new."

"Eddie didn't try it, unless he had it in this house," Daddy said, turning the page. "His parents haven't bought any groceries since they moved here."

My father had me there. My parents had been feeding them since they moved in next door. The father was an itinerant preacher from one of the extreme "Holiness" sects, who did not work a regular job. He preached that God would provide, and he was right. God had fed them well, via my father's income ever since they had moved in.

"Well, Eddie ain't the only one. All the kids around here eat 'em and everybody says they're great!"

"It's a gyp. Now go play and let me read my paper."

The first shots had been fired that night, but as far as I was concerned the battle had not begun. I fully intended to have the Phantom Spaceship card.

The next round began at breakfast. It was fairly safe since my father was at work. He would not put up with a constant nagging. I had to work through my mother.

"Why haven't you eaten your corn flakes?" Momma asked.

"I'm tired of the same old thing for breakfast. I'd like something different for a change."

"Me too. I'm tired of 'em," my brother Larry said, stuffing his mouth full of corn flakes as he spoke. He was a prodigious eater at the age of two and a half. He had already eaten two eggs that morning.

"All right," our mother said, "but it's a long time until lunch. Go on out and play."

This strategy was repeated every morning at breakfast for a week. In addition, I turned the radio up every time there was a commercial for Wheat Munchies. The big play came on Saturday, however.

My father did the grocery shopping in those days, because my mother had not yet taken up driving an automobile. We walked the aisles of the grocery stores, with Daddy reading prices closely. He was always a bargain hunter.

As we hit the cereal section, I ran ahead and stared at the hundreds of boxes of Wheat Munchies, each with a picture of the Phantom Spaceship card. Without glancing at me, my father picked up a big box of corn flakes and put them in the buggy. I held my breath.

"I want Wheat Munchies," Larry piped up from his seat in the buggy.

"What?"

"I want *Wheat Munchies*," Larry repeated, looking to me for approval.

Daddy turned to glare at me. I shrugged my shoulders and indignantly defended myself. "I didn't tell him to say it! He just likes Wheat Munchies."

Every kid with younger brothers and sisters knows that cute little kids have more influence than their older brothers and sisters. I had brainwashed Larry over the course of a week, making him repeat the phrase over and over until he had it down pat. I had whispered it to him in his sleep. I would have done the same to my sister, but she had not yet learned to talk.

"Why do you want Wheat Munchies?" Daddy asked.

"I *like* Wheat Munchies." Larry repeated the phrase like a little parrot.

"See," I said. "He *likes* Wheat Munchies."

"No! I am not gonna open the Wheat Munchies until the corn flakes are gone!" my mother said.

"Pleeeese!" I begged. It was unbearable to have the prize right there in the house without being able to get my hands on it.

"What's all this yellin'?" my father asked. If he could hear your voice in another room, you were yelling. He was the only person allowed to yell at our house.

"David wants me to open the Wheat Munchies."

An amazing thing happened. Daddy picked up the Wheat Munchies and opened them. Perhaps he had a flash of how it felt to be a small boy again. Reaching in, he handed me the card, which was encased in cellophane.

I ran to my bedroom, ripping off the wrapper, followed by Larry, who was yelling, "Let me see! Let me see!"

It was a white card. Imprinted on it was the silhouette of a black spaceship. In the center of the spaceship was a white dot. I did as the radio announcer had said. Focusing all my energy on the white dot, I suddenly looked up at the wall.

Nothing happened.

Obviously, I had not focused hard enough or glanced at the wall quickly enough. I tried it again, grunting and straining. Still nothing happened. I was thoroughly disgusted by the time my father came to my room.

"Well, did you see it?" he asked.

"No-o-o. The ship stays right on the card, no matter how hard I look at it."

"It'll always stay on the card. Lookin' hard at it is supposed to make you see it when you look somewhere else. It's what you call an optical illusion."

"It's a gyp," I moaned in disgust.

"If it's free, you can bet your money it's a gyp," my father said.

Being gypped once did not destroy my faith in Captain John of the Space Patrol. A few weeks later when the people from Wheat Munchies started advertising the Faraway Glasses, I got excited all over again.

"See for miles, just like Captain John," the radio announcer intoned. "All it takes is three Wheat Munchies box tops and twenty-five cents for handling. You too can have the Faraway Glasses delivered to your door."

The campaign for the Faraway Glasses took longer than the one to get the card. I needed three box tops from Wheat Munchies and I only had one. Worse, the first box was half full.

I immediately began to have two bowls of cereal every morning, and I pushed Larry to eat two bowls.

"They taste *awful*," he would cry.

"I know that, but don't let Momma hear you say it. I'll let you look through my Faraway Glasses when I get 'em."

"Promise?"

"Yeah, I promise." He would dig into his cereal with renewed enthusiasm.

After an eternity, during which I attempted to invite strange kids to breakfast on several occasions, we had eaten three boxes of Wheat Munchies, getting the hard part out of the way.

It only took three or four days of nagging before Momma filled out the order form and dropped the three box tops and a quarter into the mail.

"Now, it says allow four weeks for delivery," she told me. "Don't be in here every day naggin' me about it."

I nagged her for about two weeks before deciding that I was never going to get the Faraway Glasses. I was in the sandbox in the back yard when the auspicious day arrived and my mother called out to me one afternoon, less than a month later.

"Your Captain John package is here," she said from the back door.

I charged the steps, Larry in hot pursuit. With shaking hands and bated breath I ripped open the brown cardboard. I stopped breathing as the Faraway Glasses (actually goggles) came out of the wrapper.

They were of glossy black plastic, with ear pieces that wrapped around the head and a piece of black elastic to hold them in place. Slowly I slipped them on and turned to look out the door.

The entire world became a magical blur, seen through the cheap and none too clear plastic lens, which provided a little magnification but not much.

"You look jus' like Cap'n John," Larry said in awe. Neither of us had ever seen Captain John, of course, since he was a radio character, but we both knew exactly how he looked.

"Captain John of the Space Patrol!" I yelled, raising my arm dramatically. "I'm off to explore." I hurtled through the kitchen, an imaginary cape flying from my shoulders.

"David, don't run with those things on. You can't see where you're—"

Hitting the back porch on a dead run, I did not slow down. My mother was absolutely right in what she was about to say. I could not see where I was going. My legs continued to pump as I plunged into empty air off the five-foot back porch.

My face dug a furrow as I hit. My elbows and knees made separate furrows, leaving a lot of skin in the dirt. The wind was knocked completely out of me. Momma was checking for broken bones before I got my breath back. I had begun to sob by the time she started to wash my wounds.

"The Far'way Glasses broke," Larry said, extending them to me. They had broken in the middle, forever gone. I sobbed even louder as Momma advanced with the tincture of iodine to disinfect my wounds.

In a little while, I was outside showing off the broken glasses, telling my chums how I had survived a treacherous fall from the back porch. They looked at my scraped knees and elbows (wounds always looked worse with iodine on them) and wondered aloud how I had survived.

And even though they were broken, I still had the first pair of Faraway Glasses on the block. That means a lot to a small boy just turned six.

— 9 —

All the Gods Have
Feet of Clay

*P*UTTING MY BOOKS on the ground, I took
a deep breath, preparing to climb the ladder to the big slide.
Since my first day of school, two or three weeks earlier, I had
watched the more adventuresome boys in my class as they
hurtled down the "big" slide, as opposed to the "small" slide
used by the girls.

The big slide, in reality, was about eight feet high. To a
very small boy, though, it was like the peak of Everest.

Being shy and a loner by nature, I had watched from afar
as my comrades scaled the lofty heights, sliding down in the
throes of delight. Even more incredibly, one or two of them
had begun sliding down head first! They were reprimanded
each time, but they continued unabated.

Such daring caused me to lie awake at night, heart pounding at the very thought. I had determined to do it—head first
down the big slide! Not in front of others, though; no chance
of public humiliation. I would do it in secret and if I perished, my humiliation would go with me to the grave.

My only chance, I knew, would be after school. Unfortunately, Eddie, who was my next door neighbor and a year

older, had been assigned to see me home every day. Eddie was a wimp, with no adventure in his soul.

He was the perfect gentleman that all boys hate. Eddie had taken religion to heart at an early age, having caught it from his daddy, an itinerant loafer who used his church credentials as an excuse not to do anything constructive.

Once when Eddie caught me playing doctor with his sister, who was my age, he immediately snitched, getting both of us spanked. We merely moved the game elsewhere, though, making certain he did not catch us again.

"God can see you even under the house," he said when he had caught me playing with a forbidden cigarette lighter.

"*Nobody* can see through a house. Besides, God has better things to do than watch me all the time," I told him, snapping the broken Zippo.

"God *can so* see through a house. Besides, I'm gonna tell."

Deciding that I was doomed anyway, I punched Eddie in the nose, with great satisfaction. He ran home screaming and I got another spanking for "hitting first." I could defend myself (was required to do so), but "hitting first" was forbidden.

So it was on a day when Eddie was out sick that I embarked on my great adventure.

Wiping my sweaty palms on stiff, new blue jeans, I took a deep breath, swallowed hard, and began to climb. Refusing to look down from the incredible height, I pulled myself up, breathing rapidly.

At the top, I surveyed the breathtaking vista of the entire universe laid out around me: the red brick Bell Morris school, the chain-link fence out near the street, the alley and daycare center, and the firehall across the street.

Taking a breath, I plunged over, head first, to death or glory!

No roller coaster ride in later life ever thrilled my soul the way that plunge down the big slide did. Surprised to find myself alive, I caught my breath.

Smiling to myself with great satisfaction, I was contemplating doing it again, when the voice boomed out.

"Hey you!"

Looking up, my soul filled with terror. Striding toward me was a Safety Patrol boy (there were no girls in law enforcement then). There was wrath written on his brow. I knew I was about to perish. I had been caught breaking a rule by one of the elite sixth graders, wearing the white Sam Browne belt and badge.

"What?" I croaked out, looking up from my six-year-old niche in the universe to his almost omnipotent size.

"Don't you know it's against the rules to go head first down a slide?"

I shook my head, literally speechless. He took it as a denial that I knew about the rule.

"Well, it is! I guess I'll have to haul you into the principal's office. That's what happens to kids who break the rules." He was a pudgy, redheaded, freckled boy with large, protruding teeth.

The principal's office! That horrible, unspeakable place, where wayward boys went for their punishment. I had never even seen the principal, let alone his office. I imagined it to be a room with instruments of torture on the wall.

"I'll never do it again," I choked out.

"That's what they all say!"

"I promise."

"Well . . .," he paused. "Since this is the first time . . . Do you have any money?"

"Some," I answered, puzzled.

"You got a nickel for an ice cream cone?"

"I'm not allowed to stop at the ice cream shop. I hafta go straight home."

"You don't hafta stop. Give me the nickel and I don't take you in. I'll buy my own ice cream cone."

Relief flooded through me as I handed over the nickel. I would not be dragged in humiliation through the halls to the dreaded principal's office!

The Safety Patrol boy ate the first of many ice cream cones at my expense that day. The word *extortion* was not in my vocabulary, but I knew it was wrong. Unable to figure a way out, however, I went along with it. Looking back, it could not have lasted more than a few weeks, because I was only at Bell Morris school for a few months. It seemed forever, though.

Almost on a daily basis, he would be waiting, hand out as I approached his post. I came to despise him with a frustrated feeling of helplessness.

Then the hand of fate moved to free me.

"David, do you know where the principal's office is?"

My eyes widened in terror as I looked up from my drawing to my first-grade teacher. *Principal's office!* Had I been found out?

"Come out in the hall and I'll show you where it is. I want you to take a note up to the principal's secretary."

Relief! I had not been found out. Unless . . . unless it was a trick to get me there without a struggle.

"At the top of those stairs, it's on your right side. Just go to the counter and hand the lady this note."

With fear and trembling I climbed the stairs. On my right (the side opposite the small pox vaccination) I saw the counter. Approaching quietly, I extended the note to the tall lady standing there. She smiled.

"Thank you," she said. "That's a pretty sweater you're wearing."

"Yes ma'am. I have one just like it with a bare on it instead of a line." In fact, I had four animal sweaters. It was a prosperous year in the construction business. Besides the lion and the bear, I had an elephant and giraffe sweater, too.

Relieved, I turned to go. Then, hearing an angry male voice, I looked across the little swinging gate that opened beside the counter. I could see into the room at the back.

My nemesis and tormentor, the redheaded patrol boy was standing in front of a tall man with a bald head. The man's face was red.

"Don't stand there and lie to me! Two teachers watched you go through the locker and steal things. And it's not the first time! I *trusted* you! Now give me that belt and badge. You're not fit for responsibility."

The principal! I was looking at the dreaded principal. His office looked like any other office. I saw no tools of torture, not at that point anyway.

"I didn't do it," the redheaded boy said defiantly, handing him the belt and badge.

"I said, don't lie!" Suddenly the principal had him by the collar. A wooden paddle had appeared from nowhere. Bam! Bam! Bam! The principal got in three licks before the boy began to cry.

My mouth dropped open in awe. It was as if an adult were being spanked. It was as if an idol had fallen. The gigantic sixth grader, who had frightened me so badly, was whimpering and crying worse than I did when I was spanked. He had no dignity at all.

I was smiling to myself as I returned to my classroom.

"Give me my nickel." The redheaded kid extended his hand.

"No," I replied firmly.

"Whatta ya mean, no? You wanna go to the principal's office?" he asked menacingly.

"You ain't a patrol boy anymore. You was caught stealin'. If you bother me again, I'll take *you* to the principal's office and tell him you been takin' money from me."

"Oh yeah?" he screeched in impotent rage. "I'd like to see you do that. I'd just like to see it!"

Triumphant, I watched him stride angrily away. He never bothered me again.

Years later, watching as an army drill instructor stood docilely while he was thoroughly chewed out by a major, I was not too surprised. Somewhere, I knew, was a general who could do the same thing to the major.

The drill instructor was like a god to us shaven-headed recruits, but I had learned early—all the gods have feet of clay.

—10—

The Warrior King of Johnston Street

WE ALWAYS CALLED him "King" because that was what he insisted that we call him. He had a regular name, like Teddy or Bobby, but if I ever knew what it was, it is long forgotten.

King always walked around with one eye squinted almost completely closed. For a long time I thought he was blind in one eye, until I realized that he could change eyes at a moment's notice. Someone finally told me that he was imitating a movie tough guy—James Cagney, Edward G. Robinson, or one of the other stars of the era's big screen.

He was a grubby kid, always wearing what was then locally called a "polo shirt," but is now an ordinary T-shirt. His pants were regular blue jeans. High-topped black sneakers completed his wardrobe. The crowning cover of his entire costume was dirt. King was always filthy, with a black, sweaty ring around his neck. On particularly hot days, he would have several rings.

He crowned himself king because he was bigger and stronger than the rest of us. At eight or nine, he ruled a group of four-, five-, and six-year-olds. There were other older kids, I am certain, but they were occupied elsewhere and took little notice of us, except to say, "Get outta my way, Snotface," if we happened to impede them.

I came to know King only because so much of my early childhood was spent on Tennessee Avenue at my Grandparents Goin's house. They lived there at a place called "the end of the line" because Knoxville's trolley cars turned around in a field directly across the street from the house and headed back downtown. The last trolley ran three months after I was born, so I never saw one.

When Grandfather Goin was forced to sell his farm during World War II, he knew nothing of cities. He sought out the cheapest property with the most space near his new place of employment. He got the house cheap because it was in a neighborhood that could best be called "deteriorating," even in the midforties.

One block away, there was a tavern on each corner. Sometimes on Friday and Saturday nights when I was small, my Grandmother Goin and I would sit on the bank in front of the house and watch the paddy wagon load drunken brawlers. If my grandfather and Uncle A.C. were not home, Mam-maw would be especially watchful of the men being loaded.

The neighborhood was (and is) called Lonsdale, at that time an all-white, lower-working-class community. It had a fair share of street characters, who were given affectionate nicknames that would be socially unacceptable today but were used freely then as colorful and appropriate descriptions:

There was Marvalee, who had once become wedged in the door of a city bus. She was called "The Fat Woman." A retarded man named Bobby who went from house to house picking up used clothes and food was called "The Halfwit." A black man, naturally called "The Old Colored Man," went up and down the alleys in a mule-drawn wagon, collecting the slop that people set out for his pigs. And then there were numerous colorful resident "tush-hogs," an East Tennessee colloquialism for incorrigible barroom brawlers.

It was an exciting place for a little boy to live.

Johnston Street crosses Tennessee Avenue a block west of the end of the line, and King lived on Johnston Street. I never knew exactly where because I was not allowed outside a very small area that was bordered by a row of irises on one side, an apartment house on the other, an alley in the back, and a sidewalk in front. King was gone before I was big enough to leave the zone.

He ruled supreme, though, from the time I was four until I was six, which is an eternity in a child's life. Finally, a bloody and violent coup was carried out with my help by a runny-nosed little boy I remember only as Skeeter, who was somewhere near my age.

"What're y'all doin'?"

It was my first encounter with King. Most encounters that followed through the years were of a similar nature. Skeeter, myself, and several other boys were playing marbles behind my grandparents' house in the black dirt near the alley. The dirt was not black loam but was colored by a layer of soot from the nearby "acid factory," which produced sulfur (or used it for raw material). There were always piles of the yellow stuff around the plant and the smell never subsided.

"Playin' marvels," Skeeter answered, taking aim.

"That's a purty red marvel," King said, dropping to his haunches to watch, squinting maliciously with one eye.

"It's my cherry taw," Skeeter answered, blasting the marbles in the center of the ring with great skill, using his prized taw, which was what we called our shooter marble. In those days some marbles were still made from a type of stone called chert. Every male child of my acquaintance had marbles in his pocket then, and none was more prized than those we called "cherries."

Skeeter's cherry taw, I remember to this day, was an exceptional beauty, a swirling mixture of deep reds and pinks, worth fifty ordinary glass marbles for trading purposes. I was never any good at shooting but was a successful broker of marbles for many years.

"Yep. It's right purty. I think I'll just take it." King reached in and snatched up the marble.

"Hey! Gimme back my cherry taw. Who do you think you are anyway?" Skeeter stood angrily, his nose running as usual.

"I'm the king," he said. "What I say goes."

The determined Skeeter, faced with losing his prized shooter, attempted to take the marble back. King shoved him hard, sending him staggering across the yard. He laughed an ugly laugh, squinting at us through one eye.

"Any'a you little pissants wanna take me on?"

None of us did. Discretion is the better part of valor. King was at least three, maybe four years older than we were. Even the bravest of our crew was not insane.

The pattern was set. For the next two years, King terrorized me and my contemporaries. Looking back, I used to wonder why our parents did not take action. Then I realized that we never told them. In those days, at least in my environment, adults did not pry very far into the realms of their children.

As a visitor, I only had to endure King for short periods of time, but Skeeter and the others were not so fortunate. We would fantasize about his death, imagining him crushed under the wheels of a truck or eaten by a pack of wild dogs.

We all imagined his demise a thousand times, but it was the unassuming Skeeter who finally carried off the revolution—and then only because of total outrage from the straw that broke the camel's back.

"Whatcha got in the bag?" King asked.

"None of yer beeswax," Skeeter replied, pulling the brown grocery bag close to his chest. We had just come from Lanning's Grocery, a block from my grandparents' house, where we had picked up a few items for his mother.

Lanning's was the neighborhood forerunner of today's supermarkets. You could buy almost anything you needed, but you could say, "Charge it," and Mrs. Lanning would write it in "the book."

That particular day, Skeeter had added two pieces of

candy to the purchase: two-for-a-penny jawbreakers, cinnamon-flavored balls, hard as carbon steel and hot as the fires of hell. It took hours of delightful torment to suck away all the flavor, as they grew hotter with every layer that dissolved.

Skeeter was secure in his knowledge that one additional penny would not be noticed at the end of the month when his mother settled with the Lannings.

King ripped the bag from Skeeter, shoving him backward.

"Well, well, well. Two jawbreakers. One for you and one for the other pissant. I think I'll just have 'em myself, 'cause I know how hard they are to eat, and I know you little punks can't stand the heat."

He took out the two jawbreakers and handed the bag back to Skeeter. He popped one into his mouth, sneering at us and squinting through one eye, then he turned and walked away.

"Ummmmmmmmmm, good!" he said over his shoulder.

"Enough's enough!" Skeeter said through clinched teeth, as King walked away. "I'm gonna git him." We had anticipated the jawbreakers all morning.

"How? He can whip both of us at once."

"Let's take these groceries home and I'll show ya."

At home, after having his nose ritually wiped (frivolous ailments such as pollen allergies were not recognized among common people then), Skeeter led me down the alley behind Tennessee Avenue. Fearfully, I followed. At six I was straying farther than I once had, but the alley was still forbidden.

"I need a big lard can," Skeeter said, looking through the fifty-gallon drums used as garbage cans, "and there's one now."

During my childhood, lard was the exclusive cooking agent, among the poor at least. It was commonly bought in five-gallon cans. We opened it and looked at the white substance still clinging to the sides.

"This one'll do," Skeeter said.

"For what?" I asked.

"You'll see," he replied.

Half a block away, he stopped in front of a clump of

hedges. Looking both ways to make sure we were not under observation, he pointed up into the hedge.

"Look up there, in the hole."

"Holy cow!" I gasped. It was the biggest hornets' nest I had ever seen.

"Is there hornets in there?"

"Yep, and we're gonna put the nest in this lard can."

"My mom says you can die from enough hornet stings," I said.

"We ain't gonna get stung. You slip the can up over the bottom of the nest. I'll be ready with the lid. You break the limb. It's rotten anyway. I'll slap the lid on before the hornets know what's happened."

Trembling with fear, I slipped the open lard can upward over the nest, waiting for the beasties to swarm me. I was no more terrified, years later, crawling under live fire at Fort Jackson.

Reaching up, I grabbed the limb and jerked. Snap! It broke. The gray paper nest fell into the sticky lard can.

"The lid. Hurry! *They're buzzin'.*"

The intrepid Skeeter snapped the lid on and we both collapsed in relief. A vicious, throbbing hum came from the lard can, making the tin sides literally vibrate as the enraged hornets swarmed from the nest.

"We did it," I said. "Now what?"

"King goes down to the creek ever' day after lunch. He comes through the alley. We're gonna sit in your grandma's back yard with our can and shoot marvels."

"How're we gonna git him ta open it?" I asked.

"I'll handle that," Skeeter said, wiping his nose on his filthy T-shirt.

King came down the alley right on schedule, stopping from time to time to pick up a rock and hurl it at a bird. That boy was mean to the bone.

As he came near enough to see us, Skeeter got up, grabbed the lard can, and ran around behind a bush with it.

As he came back to the marble circle, King called out. Tom Sawyer couldn't have done it better.

"What's in the lard can, pissant?"

"What lard can?" Skeeter coyly asked, kneeling for a shot.

"The one you *thought* you was gonna hide from me," King said, giving us a malevolent stare through his one open eye. He walked behind the bush.

"I wouldn't open that can if I was you," Skeeter said.

"Well, you *ain't* me, pissant." King leaned forward and grasped the lid.

"I'm warnin' you for the last time," Skeeter said. By that time we were both edging toward the house, uncertain as to how wide the hornets would range when freed.

"That's right, *run!* King naturally assumed we were retreating from *his* wrath. "Go on. Git outta here you little punks!"

We ran all the way to my grandparents' back porch, then turned to watch. With a self-satisfied sneer, King looked at us and jerked the lid off.

For the first time in memory, I saw *both* King's eyes open at the same time. It was just for a moment, though, just before the angry black and white cloud of hornets engulfed him.

His screams were music to our ears as he danced like a dervish, slapping and whirling. The screams grew in volume as he turned to run down the alley toward Johnston Street, trailing a stream of angry hornets, turning into a sweet crescendo of agonized wails as he got farther away.

He had ceased to be the Warrior King and was an ordinary little boy, screaming for his mother.

"We did it," Skeeter said with a big smile.

"What if he really dies?" I asked.

"We warned him, didn't we? What else could we do? It ain't our fault that he didn't listen." Small boys sincerely believe, though they may have never heard the phrase, that "you shall reap what you sow."

Later that evening, my grandfather saw the nest, hornets

still buzzing around. He tossed gasoline on it and reduced it to ashes.

King did not die. After that day, however, he took the long way to the creek, never coming near the alley again, whether through humiliation or fear, I do not know.

Skeeter's family moved away that same year. I never forgot him though. After all, he had the idea and led the way to banishing the much-feared Warrior King of Johnston Street.

—11—

Grandmother Goin and the Obscene Machine

 MY GRANDMOTHER Goin had become an old woman while still in her fifties, at least in my memory. Her iron gray hair was braided and twisted in a tight bun on the back of her head. She wore practical black shoes, cotton dresses that buttoned up the front, and rimless glasses with metal earpieces.

I never remember seeing her dressed up, probably because she so seldom left the block on which she lived, except for the occasional family reunion back in the hills of Claiborne County.

She was four feet, eleven inches tall and weighed ninety pounds when she was a plump young girl. In her later years she was about seventy-five pounds. Born Nancy Cathryn Keck, her friends called her Cassie, or just Cass.

Her Primitive Baptist upbringing was diametrically opposed to drinking, cursing, gambling, and adultery. That was why it was such a shock when I heard her use an obscenity one day. It was such a shock that I never could remember

77

what it was that she actually said, other than the fact that it was obscene.

William Archie Gilreath, usually called W.A. by members of the Goin clan and Bill by everyone else, was my Aunt Coba's husband. In those days he was a repairman of typewriters and adding machines, among other things. From time to time he would buy a machine and resell it. It was one of those machines that caused the obscene word to come from my grandmother's mouth.

He carried it through the back door one day and put it in the alcove next to the washing machine. It was a big, heavy machine—unlike its transistorized descendants of today—with lots of colorful keys and glass and moving parts. It was a strain for one man to carry.

"W.A. (the initials were pronounced *Dub-yay*), I wish you wouldn't leave that in here." My grandmother stood in the door to the kitchen, wiping her hands on a dishtowel. "I'm afraid one of the kids will break it."

"Don't worry about it," he said. "The kids can't hurt it." He went on through the house, leaving her with a worried expression.

Sitting at the kitchen table, eating a bowl of cornbread and milk, I pretended not to have noticed the fancy machine. But as soon as Mam-maw left the kitchen, I went at it.

The adding machine was a wondrous thing. I knew it was exactly what the control panel to Captain John's spaceship had to look like. In a moment's time, I was airborne, climbing toward outer space.

Zap! Pow! Boom! Red keys, yellow keys, blue keys! I knocked over enemy ships as they hurtled at me at supersonic speeds. I had no need for electronic video games; my imagination took me anywhere I wanted to go.

I did not hear my grandmother come back into the kitchen.

"Davy, that machine is not to play with. You are the oldest grandchild (I was six then) and I expect you to help me watch it until W.A. gits it outta here."

Shamefaced, I left and found the rest of the children who were there that day: my brother and sister—Larry and Pat —and Coba and Bill's two girls—Dorothy and Sherry. Dorothy was my age and Sherry was between Pat and Larry.

Larry and Dorothy were playing Old Maid. I sat down on the floor beside them.

"You wanna play?" Dorothy asked.

"Naw. I've been playin' spaceship."

There was no response. They went on with the game.

"It's like real spaceship controls," I continued.

"What's like real spaceship 'trols?" Larry asked, trying to match Little Bo Peep with Mary and her Little Lamb.

"I *told* you, you can't put Bo Peep and Mary together!" Larry, then three, reluctantly picked them back up.

"The machine W.A. put in the kitchen," I explained.

"What machine?" Dotty asked, drawing the Old Maid from Larry, who giggled out loud.

"The machine with all the buttons," I answered.

"Yeah, I seen that in the car," Dotty replied.

"I wanna see it," Larry said, getting up, leaving the cards on the floor.

"We're not finished," Dotty objected. "I'm stuck with the Old Maid!"

"You lose, you lose," Larry yelled over his shoulder.

Dorothy laid her cards down and followed the rest of us as we trooped through the kitchen. Our grandmother was not in sight.

Larry ran to the machine, tripped, and slammed his head. He was always doing that. The machine jingled and jangled loudly, bringing Mam-maw from the bedroom just off the kitchen.

She stood, lips pursed for a moment, but remained calm.

"All of you listen. That machine is very expensive. It is not to play with. Do y'all understand?"

We all nodded that we understood, each plotting and planning ways to get at it when no adult was in sight. It was the first of many hundreds of times that our grandmother warned us about the adding machine.

It was to become the bane of her life for the next few months.

"Johnny Ray," grandmother yelled, "git off that cheer and leave my canaries alone."

"I wanna see the aigs," Johnny Ray, four years old, said.

"If you disturb 'em, they'll never hatch the aigs! Git down, before I blister your hiney!"

Mam-maw stood behind her wringer-type washer, squeezing the laundry through it. If there were automatic washers then, the poor knew nothing of them. It was wash, rinse, then through the wringer.

It was cold out, so she was stuck in the house with six grandkids that day, ranging from six to eighteen months or so. I don't remember why we were all there.

"Mam-maw, Larry is tryin' to play the organ again." Dorothy stood in the kitchen door, hands on hips.

The old bellows-type organ had always fascinated Larry. It had pedals to pump, knobs to pull, and a stool that would spin in circles. It was almost as intriguing as the adding machine.

With a sigh, our grandmother went to get him away from the antique organ. She had no sooner left than Johnny Ray was back on the chair, trying to get at the canary cage again. Pat and Sherry were at the adding machine, punching buttons.

"Y'all better behave," I wisely told them, "or you're gonna be in trouble."

"That does it!" Grandmother Goin said, coming from the bedroom with Larry under her arm. Setting him down, she grabbed Johnny Ray and tried to swat his bottom. He began to yell and put his hands in her way. Pat and Sherry ran away from the adding machine. In the bedroom, Dorothy began to play the organ.

"I'm goin' out to hang up the wash. All of you sit here at the table and eat your cookies. I'd better not catch you into mischief when I come back in," she warned, putting on her coat and head scarf.

We all nodded understanding and watched her pick up the metal washtub and carry it out the back door; then we scrambled over to the adding machine.

"We'll take turns watchin' out the window for her," I said. "You watch first, Larry."

"Why do I always hafta watch first?"

"Just do it!" I replied. The rest of us crowded around and began to enthusiastically punch the keys.

"She's comin'," Larry whispered a few minutes later.

When she came in, we were all back at the table, smiling like little angels. She looked at us suspiciously but loaded up another tub of wet clothes and went back out.

"It's your turn to watch, Pat," I told her.

Not quite two, she nodded assent and toddled over to the window. Standing on her toes, she looked out. Soon we were all engrossed again in the hundreds of colored buttons—including Pat, who forgot all about looking out the window.

The cold draft alerted us that we had been caught. We stampeded back to the kitchen and turned. Grandmother Goin stood quietly for a moment, a little elf of a woman.

Putting the basket down, she took off her cloth coat and head scarf. Turning slowly, she walked toward the big adding machine with the menacing stride of an Old West gunfighter stepping onto a dusty street.

It was a complete shock when her black lace-up shoe connected with it the first time. Glass flew everywhere.

"I've told him . . ." she kicked it again, "a thousand times . . ." another kick "to get this *blankety-blank* machine out of here!"

Total silence fell as the word (whatever it was) came out of her mouth. Pieces of the machine settled in the floor and she turned slowly toward us.

"I reckon I won't have to worry about you kids breakin' this machine anymore, will I?"

When W.A. came to pick up Dorothy and Sherry that afternoon, he stopped and looked at the glass and metal parts on the floor. We had not been near the machine, or even in the room again, not after what we had witnessed.

"What happened?" he asked.

"Mam-maw flew at it an' kicked it apart," Dorothy said in a breathless and awe-stricken voice. "And she *cussed* while she was doin' it."

Without a word, he picked the broken machine up and carried it out to the car. To my knowledge, he never brought it up with my grandmother.

It was probably the best thing he could have done, under the circumstances. You should never cross a Primitive Baptist once she gets to the cussing point.

—12—

A Little Farm on Rifle Range Road

My FATHER ALWAYS wanted to be a farmer. I think it was because his idea of bucolic country living was as far removed from his brutal, urban childhood existence as anything he could imagine.

He died, still burning with shame at having been raised in rundown clapboard houses in the slums. He once told me that his family moved every time the rent was due and that they were not "the Hunters," but "*The* Hunters."

When I was six, my dad bought his "farm," one and a quarter acres on a gravel, semirural road. He always referred to it as "my little farm on Rifle Range Road."

On this estate was a four-room house with no bathroom. Poor as we were, we had always had a bathroom, though outhouses were still common in rural areas. I, however, was delighted when first introduced to the little wooden building out back. It was a one seater, as opposed to more luxurious units.

At six, I thought it was simply marvelous.

"Guess what?" I asked a gathering of family, not long after we moved to Rifle Range Road. They all turned to listen. "Our new house ain't got a bathroom. You hafta go *outside.*"

My embarrassed father quickly explained that it was a temporary matter. True to his word, his little farm soon had not only an indoor bathroom but also livestock.

"Let me go after Bessie," I implored.

"No," my father said, pouring the slop for his two grunting pigs, Petunia and Pinky.

On his one-and-a-quarter-acre farm, he eventually accumulated two pigs, fifty chickens, a cow, a vegetable garden, two rabbits (my responsibility) and a small barn he had constructed from trees he cut himself. He had determined to farm, no matter how much it cost him.

We made butter from the milk, but the milk itself was given to a poor family nearby. City kids that we were, none of us would drink "raw" milk. We also gave away a lot of eggs.

"Why not? The kids next door go after their cow, and they're *girls.*"

"They're also older and bigger than you are. You can't handle that cow."

"Yes I can."

Daddy stopped what he was doing and turned to look at me. He was dark and swarthy, with massive arms and shoulders, already going gray at twenty-seven. He saw a skinny little boy with blond hair and silver-gray eyes. Most Hunters are skinny until we hit adulthood.

"All right," he said, "go get your coat on. It's getting chilly. You think you can do it; go ahead and get Bessie. So help me, though, you'd *better not* let my cow get away." He did not specify the punishment for such an offense.

Literally leaping for joy, I ran into the house to put my coat on. It was real leather, with a fur collar and a baseball-type cap with ear flaps to match. It was also very expensive, bought because I had been so entranced by it.

In that coat and hat I became Sergeant Preston of the Yukon, doing missions for the government. The story was forming in my mind, even as I prepared to fetch the cow. In my scenario, a giant, maddened bull had escaped and was ravaging the countryside. It was my assignment to bring it in alive.

"Where are you goin'?" my mother asked.

"To get Bessie," I replied, after taking only a moment to shift back to reality.

"I don't think—" she began.

"Daddy said I could."

"All right. Be careful," she conceded, wiping her hands on a dishtowel. My mother did not interfere in "man things." Years later, when the pain of growing up brought me into conflict with my father, she would tell me that he did not mean to hurt me with his gruff ways, but she never spoke a word against him.

Bessie was staked out on a chain a few hundred yards up the road, behind a wooded area, there not being enough grass on our miniature farm to feed her. We rented the field from someone else.

Minutes later, Sergeant Preston of the Yukon crept up on the monstrous bull with foam dripping from its mouth and unhooked the chain from the stake in the ground. Old Bessie, cropping grass, calmly surveyed me. She knew it was time to go home for sweet corn and the relief of milking.

"All right, varmint," I yelled to the wild bull, "let's go. You'll frighten no more settlers tonight." I yanked the chain. Bessie turned and began to walk away. She knew that the shortest distance between two points is a straight line. The straight line was through the thick woods.

"Whoa!" I yelled. "*This* way!" I dug in my heels, but she pulled me along at the end of the chain. Then she began to trot, faster and faster.

"Whoa, you stupid cow!"

Sergeant Preston stayed on his feet until the wild bull reached a full run, then his six-year-old legs could no longer keep up. I lost my footing and went down on my face. It was a slow motion nightmare.

Across the grass, into the woods. Sergeant Preston returned to the Yukon as a cow dragged a terror-stricken six-year-old through the blackberry patches, across old logs and stumps, and over rocks.

My hands tightened as the chain began to slip painfully through them.

"*You'd better not let my cow get away.*" The words echoed in my mind as I was dragged through the woods.

Upon reaching the embankment above the road, Bessie jumped the few feet to the road. I almost lost my grip as I plunged downward. The wind was painfully knocked from me. Then I was on the gravel road, turning over and over on the rocks as the cow picked up speed again.

We went down the driveway, past the front porch where my mother, little sister, and brother stood watching. My father turned in the chicken lot as we went by. Finally, Bessie reached the barn and stopped.

In a few moments, Daddy was prying my white, bleeding knuckles from the chain. My leather jacket and cap were in shreds. My face and hands were covered with scratches, my palms blistered from friction, and my pants were in rags.

"I brought Bessie home," I gasped.

"Yes, you did." He picked me up gently and brushed me off.

"Go to the house and let your mother clean you up. You done good."

A few tears escaped my eyes as I walked to the house, but I did not let anyone see them. Nor did I cry when the antiseptic was being applied as my brother Larry stood in awe while I was being treated.

I had brought the cow home. My father, sparse with his praise, said I had "done good." Sergeant Preston of the Yukon could not have done better.

The expensive leather jacket, hanging in tatters, was never mentioned.

—13—

How I Learned to Read in a Day

*T*HE PRINCIPAL OF Halls Elementary spoke in a low voice to the first-grade teacher, Mrs. Corum, while glancing at me from the corner of his eye.

Adults always think that children either do not listen or do not understand what is being said. Otherwise, they would not say such cruel things in front of them.

"I hate to do this to you in midterm," he said, "but you have the most room. This child is apparently retarded. He hasn't even learned to print his name in four months.

"The note from his last teacher says he isn't capable of learning anything. I know you already have one retarded child in your class, but I can't help it."

In those days, even educators minced no words.

When he had gone, Mrs. Corum and the teacher with whom she shared a room (there were double shifts of students at the time) took me outside.

"David," Mrs. Corum asked, "what is your full name?"

"William David Hunter," I replied.

"How old are you?"

"Six."

"Do you have brothers and sisters?"

"Uh huh. A brother and a sister. They don't go to school yet."

"Where do you live?"

"On Rifle Range Road, in Knoxville, Tennessee."

"What kind of games do you play?"

"I like to play Captain John of the Space Patrol and sometimes the Lone Ranger," I said. "My little brother is sometimes Tonto, my faithful Indian companion."

"There's nothing wrong with this child," Mrs. Corum said sharply. "We'll start him out in the Cars and see what happens."

The class was divided into Cars, Trains, and Airplanes, with each child represented by a symbol on the wall: green cars, brown trains, and blue airplanes, each with a child's name on it.

There were no bones about fast, medium, and slow in those days. There were few Cars or Airplanes; most were in the middle group, the Trains.

My first morning as a Car was a disaster. I sat silent when asked to read the simplest words and stared at the paper when asked to copy from the board, as I had done for the previous four months. When I attempted to draw on the writing paper, Mrs. Corum firmly stopped me.

"There is a time for drawing and a time for lessons, David. In this class, we do them at the proper time."

I had done nothing but draw since my first day of school. The young teacher at Bell Morris, whose name I no longer remember, had never been able to stop me. She would tell me that I "should" listen in reading group, and that I "shouldn't" spend the day drawing, but she never spoke absolutely. As a result, I spent all my days drawing while my fellow students worked.

"David," Mrs. Corum said, "this is your second day. You have some catching up to do. This is Jackie. She is going to be your tutor. That means she's going to help you learn to read."

Jackie was a pigtailed little girl, boney-kneed, with both

front teeth missing. She smiled at me shyly. In the back of the room, in a quiet nook, she began.

"This is the alphabet," she piped out. "This is an *a* and this is—"

"b, c, d, e, f, g, h, i, j, k, l, m, n, o, p, q, r, s, t, u, v, w, x, y, z," I said with a smile.

"I thought you didn't know your letters?" Jackie asked accusingly.

Shrugging, I looked at her. No one had asked me if I knew my letters. Maybe I hadn't known until that very moment that I knew the alphabet. I certainly didn't know that I could read, though I had been doing it since I was three. I had learned by demanding that someone read the newspaper comic strips to me every day as soon as the paper arrived, beginning when I was still in diapers. Ernie Bushmiller's *Nancy* was my favorite.

As time passed, I was reading ahead of whoever was holding me in their lap. By the time I knew I was doing it, I thought everyone did it.

Sitting in my first classroom, with a well-meaning but inept teacher, I made absolutely no connection between the newspapers and the hard-cover books. Words were in little balloons, issuing from the mouths of cartoon characters. They were relevant.

"Do you know this word?" Jackie asked.

"No."

"It's your name. D-A-V-I-D."

I sat staring at her, perplexed, still not comprehending.

"Say it," Jackie told me, but still I sat in silence.

"If you don't try, you'll never even be able to read a newspaper."

Newspaper! Comic strips! The synapses connected. A veil was pulled away. Enlightenment had come!

"I don't guess I even need to ask if you know *this* word," she said in her little girl voice, pointing to the page.

"House," I said confidently.

Looking at me suspiciously, she pointed again.

"Car. The car is red. The house is white," I said with a smile.

In a few minutes I was reading, stumbling only over unfamiliar words, such as proper names. I understood, at last, that the words in the book were exactly the same as the words in the newspaper I had been reading for years. As soon as Jackie showed me how to sound out the syllables, I had no trouble with even unfamiliar words.

We moved quickly through the Cars reading book, then through the Trains reading book. We were into the Airplanes book when Mrs. Corum noticed us.

"Jackie," Mrs. Corum said, "I told you to start with the Cars reading book. A child has to learn the simple things first. Go back to your seats. That's enough for today."

"Don'tcha wanna hear him read?"

"Jackie, we must take this slowly." It was obvious that the veteran teacher did not want me embarrassed.

"But he *can* read," Jackie said.

"Jackie, honey, I know you want to help, but nobody learns to read in a couple of hours."

"He did," Jackie said stubbornly. I nodded my head affirmatively, smiling.

"All right," the teacher smiled gently, "go ahead and show me what you've learned today."

"See Dick and Jane," I said. "See baby Sally. See Spot run. Spot has a ball. Spot has a red ball—"

"Wait," Mrs. Corum interrupted, removing the book from my hand. She apparently thought I had memorized the first few pages. Taking a piece of paper, she began to print on it. In a minute she handed it to me.

"Read this," she said.

I adjusted to the change from book to paper and began to read. "My name is David. I live in a house. I live in a good house. I am . . ." I stumbled over a new word, then puzzled it out, "six years old."

"Come with me, David. Jackie, you may go to your seat."

In a few minutes, I was reading for a puzzled principal. Mrs. Corum spent the next few days talking about the miracle of the child who learned to read in one day. I never

bothered to tell anyone any differently—even when I realized, years later, what had happened.

I sometimes shudder to think what might have been, if I
had stayed with that first teacher. Tell any child that something is wrong with him, tell him often enough, and he'll believe it.

A good teacher is a pearl without price.

—14—

The Bare-Bottomed King of the Chicken Lot

WHEN MY FATHER set out to do something, he never did it halfheartedly. So having decided to raise chickens, he drove to the country (the real country) in search of stock.

Being a habitual bargain hunter, he shopped at numerous farms, comparing prices. Finally he found what, in his opinion, was the most for the least. He returned home that afternoon and backed our 1952 green-and-beige Studebaker into the lot he had fenced in earlier, opened the trunk, and began to shoo the chickens out. He had driven across two counties with all those white leghorns thrashing about the trunk—twenty-five or so hens and a giant rooster.

As the chickens hit the ground, expressing total indignation at their treatment, my brother Larry, who was three at the time, made an astute observation: "Them chickens ain't got no feathers on their butts."

"They don't," Momma said, holding my little sister on her hip.

Of course, I began to giggle, which reduced Larry to hysterics and made our mother try to hide her own grin. Daddy was serious about his little farm on Rifle Range Road. It was funny, though, that entire flock of chickens with no tail feathers whatsoever; just big bare bottoms.

"Is it the breed?" Momma asked, snickering.

"No, they're white leghorns," Daddy said, somewhat sheepishly. "The farmer says they have some kind of chemical deficiency. They eat each others' feathers."

Indeed, as we watched, one hen walked over behind another and plucked out a feather. The victim leaped away squawking, then immediately repeated the process on another hen.

"Well, I know they lay eggs," my father said. "I saw the eggs in their nests when I picked 'em up. That's the important thing."

Whatever the problem was, my father was never able to cure it. He bought every manner of vitamin and mineral supplement known to man and he coated their bare rear-ends with everything from axle grease to mange cures, but the chickens kept their bare bottoms as long as we owned them.

"That rooster's a mean one," Momma said, putting my sister Pat down to toddle in the grass. She was staring into the lot.

"Naw, he's just doin' his job," Daddy replied.

At that moment there was a yelp of pain from our mongrel dog, Butch. We turned in time to see the dog streaking across the chicken lot, the bare-bottomed rooster in hot pursuit. My father opened the gate. Butch hurtled through and did not stop until he was on the other side of the house. It was his last foray into the chicken lot.

"The dog was an animal intruder," my father said. "The rooster won't bother people."

We watched the rooster stick out his chest as he stared at the retreating dog, then immediately mount one of his flock—a thoroughly ridiculous-looking, but undisputed king.

★   ★   ★

Daddy's prediction proved wrong, I found out that same afternoon. My favorite place to play was a little barn he had built with his own hands. Inside, I was Davy Crockett at the Alamo or Prince Valiant, defending my castle from the barbarians. Adults seldom intruded there.

In order to arrive at the barn, I had to cross the rooster's domain. He immediately confronted me and began to strut out a challenge. I was carrying a broomstick sword/long rifle, with which I swatted at him. He danced out of the way and ran at me again, squawking violently.

City-raised though I was, a rooster's spurs were no mystery. For the uninitiated, roosters have a horny growth on the back of their legs, just above the feet, called spurs. The rooster uses them as weapons. Flying at an opponent, he raises his legs and strikes with them. Gamecock fighters strap razors to the spurs, which cause fatal combat. Even an ordinary rooster, however, can draw blood with his stock equipment.

I took to my heels, seeing instantly that the rooster was not impressed by my puny stick. Hoisting myself over the wire fence, I could hear my adversary gaining on me as I landed on the other side.

Thereafter, it was necessary for me to find the rooster busy elsewhere, then run at breakneck speed to the barn. After his first encounter with my father, the rooster generally left adults alone. Daddy had drop-kicked the fowl about fifteen feet the first time he attempted an attack.

The big bird made an exception to the adult rule one morning when he caught my mother bent over in the cramped hen house, collecting breakfast eggs.

As the monster bird flew at her face, spurs raised, she abruptly backed up, driving a nail that was protruding from the wall into the fleshy part of her buttocks.

"That rooster has to go!" Momma announced, limping into the kitchen with a basket of eggs. "He's vicious!"

"Naw," Daddy replied. "He's just doin' his job." We all knew by then that he had a sneaking admiration for the big rooster. He boasted to the neighbors that he had the "toughest leghorn in Tennessee." A few neighbors had even brought in their own champions to try him out. Everyone laughed at the bare bottom, but our rooster always emerged victorious.

He might have lived a long and prosperous life, had he not done the unthinkable.

One of the things I had hit upon to amuse myself that year involved Larry. Three years younger than me, I was his idol while we were growing up. No matter how many times I played tricks on him, he always forgave and was ready for more.

Anyone else who attempted such shenanigans would find himself on the receiving end of my fiercely protective wrath. Only I was allowed to harass my cotton-topped little brother.

"I'm openin' the gate. Are you ready?" I'd say.

"Are you sure the rooster ain't watchin'?" Larry would fearfully ask.

"Naw," I would reply, perfectly aware that the alert leghorn *was* watching with his baleful black eyes. The bird would start walking in our direction the moment that gate swung open. As soon as we were a hundred or so feet inside his domain, I would turn and run back to the gate and close it behind me.

My sudden outburst of speed would cause the rooster to squawk and hurtle toward my brother, who would go into hysterics and pound back to the gate on his chubby little legs, the bird in hot pursuit.

"Open the gate! Open the gate!" Larry would scream. Then, just as the rooster was about to overtake him (at the last possible second), I would let him out. The rooster would strut back and forth, scratching and clucking to show his grandeur. I would laugh hysterically as my brother recovered from the treachery.

One summer day, Larry decided to have a laugh on someone else, that someone being our little sister Pat, who was then still a toddler. Unfortunately, Pat could not outrun the

rooster and Larry was not big enough to manage the gate
with sufficient speed.

Our mother was sitting on the front porch, reading the
newspaper that day, and I was on the ground, shooting marbles. Larry came around the corner of the house and stood
with his head down, rubbing his bare foot back and forth.

"Momma," he mumbled.

"What?" she laid the paper aside.

"Me and Pat were goin' down to the barn." Larry never
did jump right into a story. He always built it a little at a
time.

"You know you're not supposed to go into that chicken lot
alone. Where's Patty?"

"Right here," he nodded his head to the side.

"Is she all right?" my mother asked in alarm.

"Yeah," Larry said, pursing his lips, "but the rooster did
spur her just a *little*." He reached and got her by the arm.

Just then Pat stepped around the house, a brown-haired
toddler, barefoot and wearing only white cotton panties. She
was covered with blood from her neck to her knees. Perfectly
calm, she had not even cried.

"Oh Lord!" Momma ran to Pat, snatched her up, and
rushed inside.

Larry looked back at me as I stared at him with a horrible
realization coming over me. I was certain that *my* sins were
going to be brought out.

"I couldn't get the gate opened back quick enough," he
said by way of explanation.

The wounds were all superficial, about like fingernail
scratches. Momma never got around to asking how Pat had
become locked into the lot, and Pat was too young to tell the
story.

When our father came home that evening, Momma was
waiting. "I told you that rooster was dangerous! Look what
he's done to Pat." She held the little girl up, Band-aids and all.

Without a word, Daddy went to the hall closet and took
out his Mossberg .22 caliber rifle. It only came out for

chicken hawks or other varmints. He walked to the back porch, loading it and looking grim.

To this day I believe that the story would have been different had the rooster spurred me or my brother. Our father would have chastised us for carelessness and told us that the wounds were minor. But the rooster had attacked his daughter. In the South, especially in those days, no living creature molested a man's little girl and got away with it.

On the back porch, he raised the rifle and took aim. The giant rooster with the bare bottom was striding about, surveying his domain, unaware that Judgment Day was upon him.

Crack! For a moment, I thought he had missed. The big bird appeared startled for a second, half-turned, walked a few steps, then fell over.

The saga had ended. No one even suggested to Daddy that we might eat his rooster. The people next door had him for Sunday dinner only because our father didn't believe in wasting food.

Later, he would say, "For a second there, I thought that rooster was gonna grab his chest and say, 'Why did you shoot me, Bill?'"

—15—

Pinky Pig and the Tenderloin

*P*INKY WAS A black and white pig, with a pink nose, who grew into a large hog. He had arrived in the company of a white pig, who was christened Petunia, but one day my mother found her stumbling around, unable to see. She died the next day.

Old-timers in the neighborhood listened to the sow's symptoms and said that she had "eaten glass." So Pinky grew up as an only pig on our father's acre-and-a-quarter farm.

Being an only pig, Pinky ate well. In addition to a mixture of stale bread and mash, he also ate a lot of table scraps. No matter how busy he was, though, he always had time for conversation with me.

"You're lookin' good today, Pinky," I would say.

He would look up from his trough, slop clinging to the end of his sensitive nose, raise his ears, and grunt a reply to everything I said to him.

When he was through eating, he would rare up on the wooden sides of his pen, front feet over the top rail, for a scratching between his ears. He would close his eyes with a contented sigh and enjoy the sensation, grunting with pleasure. As he got older, I would use a stick to scratch his back and he would drift off to sleep, sighing contentedly.

There was not a mean bone in Pinky's body. Sometimes our mongrel dog, Butch, would climb into the pen and eat with him. Pinky always shared well. Sometimes they would sleep, nose to nose, after a good meal—the sleep of the innocent.

A pig's life (at least that of one intended for the table) is measured only in months, but six months in the life of a small boy is an eternity. It seemed that Pinky and I had been friends forever when the first cold snap of October came.

My Grandfather Goin had come weeks earlier to the house. He and my father converted the space under the back porch to a storage shed and stacked bags of salt in there. I don't recall that I ever asked what would be stored there.

It was a Saturday in November, when I awoke to the sound of a squealing hog. Going outside on the front porch in my bare feet, I saw my father and our neighbor from across the road bringing a large white hog down the driveway at the end of a rope. The hog was not going gentle into his good night.

"What's goin' on?" I yelled to my Grandfather Goin, who was standing by the driveway watching as the hog was dragged by.

A tall, gray, and slow-moving man, he turned. "It's hog killin' day," he said. "I'm here to help your daddy. He's never butchered a hog before."

Satisfied, I went in for breakfast. My Grandmother Goin, all four feet eleven, eighty pounds of her, was putting a plate of eggs and bacon on the table. My mother was washing out several big metal cans.

"What're those for?" I asked.

"Lard," my grandmother answered. "We're killin' hogs today. Set down and eat breakfast."

I did so, watching the activities with interest. At six, I was aware of the elemental laws of life. On more than one occasion, I had seen my farm-raised mother, who detested violence, wring a chicken's neck without thinking twice.

She would grab the startled bird and swing it with a snap

of the wrist. The head would be left in her hand as the body hit the ground, sometimes running around on reflex—which is responsible, I'm sure, for the origin of the phrase "running around like a chicken with its head cut off."

It did not occur to me, however, that Pinky would be involved in the day's activities. After all, I had seen the white hog brought in. I assumed he would be the guest of honor.

Having been told to stay inside, I wandered to my bedroom and looked out the window. A black cast-iron pot was hanging over a fire. The pot would be used to render, or melt, fat into lard.

Near the barn, I saw my grandfather spreading corn on the ground. The white hog was following, snapping up the grain as he was led to open ground. Finally, Pa-paw made a little pile and the pig stopped to gulp it down.

Daddy appeared with his Mossberg .22 rifle and knelt in front of the hog, taking dead aim. I heard the crack of the small-caliber round. The big white hog shook its head once, then went back to eating. It was not until the third shot that it toppled over and died.

Since I did not know the hog personally, the death scene looked like an abstract picture to me.

Losing interest, I went to the living room and turned on the radio. Soon I was listening to *The Teddy Bear Hour* and *The Buster Brown Show.*

It was two hours or so later when Mam-maw called out to me.

"David, do you want a tenderloin sammich?" I never heard either of my grandparents say "sandwich." It was a part of the Claiborne County dialect, which also spoke of "chimbleys" and "cheers," rather than chimneys and chairs.

"What's a tenderloin?" I asked, going into the kitchen. Whatever it was, my little brother was already munching away. "It's the best part of a hog," she said, "and it's never better than when it's fresh."

"All right." I climbed up on a chair and ate not one, but two tenderloin sandwiches, thinking how nice our neighbor was to give us part of his hog.

After we had eaten, Larry and I retreated to our bedroom and strapped on six-guns. For the next two hours, we were western good guys and bad guys by turns, fighting numerous duels. We killed and were killed in gun battle after gun battle, ignoring the goings-on outside our room.

Tiring of the game, we went to the kitchen for something to drink. Halfway across the kitchen, I stopped in horror. Raising my hand, I could only point.

In a metal tub, sitting in the center of the floor, Pinky's head—bristles scalded away—sat staring into eternity.

"What's wrong?" my mother asked, seeing my pale complexion.

"It's Pinky," I finally gasped out.

"You *knew* we were killing hogs today. That's why Mr. Carr brought his hog down. That's why your Pa-paw is here to help your daddy."

"Pinky's not a *hog*, he's a pig. He was my pig!"

"He's a dead pig now," my brother said, staring in fascination.

"We thought you understood," Momma told me, as I stared in horror at Pinky's head.

"What're you gonna do with the head?" Larry asked, walking over for a better look. He had not been close to Pinky.

"We'll use it for souse meat," Mam-maw replied. Souse meat is also called "head cheese." Ground up and highly spiced, it is much like liverwurst.

In my bedroom, I sat and trembled. It was perhaps the first time I became really aware that all living things will one day cease to exist. It also brought home the horrible fact that trust, for Pinky certainly trusted us to care for his needs, is not enough to get you through.

Fortunately, it was several weeks before I realized the true source of the tenderloin sandwiches I had gobbled down.

Sometimes I will still have a piece of tenderloin at a country restaurant. It never fails, though, that I flash back to a morning in early autumn, so many years ago, and think of Pinky, staring at me from the washtub.

Being a rational adult, though, I only shudder a little, then go back to my meal.

—16—

The Resurrected Chicken

*T*HAT'S RIGHT," Tony said, "pound real hard on the edges and it'll get sharp as a razor."

Tony was a transplanted Chicago street kid, a year older than my seven years. As he instructed me in the art of making lethal arrows, he was eating a watermelon. It was one of my father's failures on his acre-and-a-quarter farm.

My Grandfather Goin had told him that the soil was not right for watermelons, but he had planted a row anyway. None had gotten larger than a baseball.

My brother and I had been warned not to eat them, but Tony would eat anything that did not bite him first. It was the result of being hungry often, but I did not know that then. To me, the wiry little boy with big eyes was just an interesting person from another universe called Chicago, Illinois.

"It's gettin' sharp," I said, holding my arrow up to look at the edge. It was a reed, of a variety that abounded in the fields around the house. It grew straight and dried hard. Around the end, I had pounded a cap from a soft drink bottle. It was, indeed, sharp on the edge and the point.

We had gotten out of sight behind the barn to manufacture the tools of death and destruction. My parents had never specifically told me *not* to make potentially lethal arrows from reeds and bottle caps, but somehow I knew they would not approve.

Our bows were green saplings with butcher string holding them taut. The string would stretch after a while, making it necessary to throw another loop around the top, bending the sapling a little farther each time, until finally it lost the ability to bend. We were usually gone to another game before that happened.

"You think it'll kill a rabbit?" I asked my mentor.

"It'll kill a grizzly bear," he assured me.

"I didn't know we was goin' bare huntin'," Larry, then pushing four, said. "Bares are big."

"Don't worry," Tony assured him, "we probably won't see any bears. If we do, though, I can grin 'em down like Davy Crockett. Might see a deer, though." There wasn't a deer in twenty miles, or a bear in fifty, but reality never disturbs small boys.

"Deers has big sharp horns," Larry said.

"Are you scared?" Tony asked sneeringly.

"He ain't skeered. He's just never been huntin' for big game," I quickly cut in, before an argument could erupt. I was enjoying the game and did not want to fight with Tony. Only I was allowed to push my little brother around. Everyone else had to walk over me first. Besides, I suspected that Tony was tough.

He said he was, anyway.

"Well, we got three arrows now," Tony said. "I'm ready to go out hunting."

"We're in big trouble if Momma catches us outside the fence," Larry predicted.

"She ain't gonna catch us 'cause she's got company. Besides, we'll be outta sight behind the barn," I told Larry.

"Yeah, and she wouldn't recognize you in your disguise, even if she did see ya," Tony reassured him.

All of us were bare-chested, with old neckties around our

heads for headbands and chicken feathers sticking from them. Tennis shoes and shorts completed the costume.

The intended hunting grounds lay between our back fence and the woods on the other side of the field. There were perhaps ten acres of woodland, which to a seven-year-old boy was like the Great Smoky Mountains National Park. There were mysteries in those woods.

We crawled under the wire fence, keeping a sharp eye out for the old man who lived across the field. Legend had it that he was 150 years old and had arrived on a wagon train.

He had once called my mother because I was annoying his cows with a homemade peashooter. A bent old man with a shock of white hair, he would sometimes walk the boundaries of his farm. He carried a cane with a dog's head carved on the top.

We walked across the open field, Indian-style, bent over at the waist, almost covered by the grass around us.

"Hold it, braves," Tony yelled. "There's a giant beast in front of us. Get ready!" He strung his bow. Larry and I followed suit, spying the beast ahead. It was a big toad.

"Ready! Shoot!"

We let fly the arrows, which landed all around the toad, but did not touch it. The beast changed directions and hopped lazily away. Twice more we sent our shafts after him, leaving him unscathed.

We could have run right up on him, of course, ensuring a kill, but that would have been a violation of the code. Finally, we lost sight of him.

We had no more success with a covey of quail and a lone blue jay. After a while we sat down in the dirt.

"Well, Geronimo," Tony said to me, "it looks like we go hungry tonight. Dark is coming."

"You speak true, Runnin' Deer. The Great Spirit has not smiled on us. We'll have to eat white man's food tonight."

"What's white man's food?" Larry asked.

"White man's food comes from a can, Little Horse," I told him.

"My name's not Little Horse; it's Flyin' Eagle. I changed it," he announced indignantly.

"Sorry, Flyin' Eagle," I told him.

"Look!" Running Deer said. "Giant birds. Much meat."

The chickens from the old man's farm were flying up to roost in the lower tree limbs of the nearby woods. His chickens were not kept up. He collected enough eggs for his own use; the rest either fed the animals of the field or produced chicks.

"We'd better leave them alone," I said. "If the old man sees us, he'll call my momma. He's done it before."

"Aw, come on," Running Deer said, "*one* shot. We probably won't hit 'em anyway."

"All right. *One* shot," I agreed.

We crept up to the trees, putting our arrows in our bows. "Let fly!" Running Deer yelled.

The arrows arched toward the tree. Running Deer's went over the chickens. Flying Eagle's shaft fell short. I watched in horror as my arrow embedded itself in the plump breast of a Rhode Island Red hen. She fluttered from the tree squawking.

"Run!" Running Deer yelled.

We took to our heels in terror. Small boys always believe that they are being watched. As we crawled under the fence, we were waiting for the old man to yell at us.

"You're gonna be in trouble," Larry gasped.

"I've gotta get home before it gets too dark," Tony said, abandoning us.

The next twenty-four hours of my life were lived in mortal terror, a type of terror known only to small boys and convicted murderers. My father, I knew, would kill me when he found out what I had done. He would kill me in spite of my mother's pleas for mercy.

All day I sat at my desk in school, waiting for the police to walk through the door of Mrs. Barker's second-grade class. They would have shotguns and handcuffs. It had dawned on me by that time that what I had done was not only the type of crime punishable by parents, but also the type of thing that put cops like Sgt. Joe Friday of the Los Angeles Police Department on your tail.

Arriving at home that afternoon, I squared my shoulders and walked in, certain the old man would be waiting with his wooden cane. Larry, waiting on the front porch, gave me a look of sympathy. He could afford it. We knew where the blame would fall, where it always fell—squarely on the shoulders of the firstborn.

In the kitchen a pot of pinto beans was simmering on the stove. A pan of cornbread was waiting for the beans. Green onions and sliced tomatoes (two of my father's agricultural successes) were on a plate.

The scene appeared perfectly normal. I knew better, though. What was about to happen was so horrible that Momma could not bring herself to mention it. I changed my clothes and went out, Larry tagging along behind me.

"Don't go far. Supper's ready and your daddy'll be home in a few minutes," Momma called.

"Look!" Larry said as we walked toward the barn, across the lot where a white leghorn rooster with a bare butt had once reigned supreme.

A thrill of terror shot through me. The old man was in the field beside the fence, leaning on his cane and looking at his small flock of semiwild chickens. My throat locked in panic.

The big red hen I had slain was walking around with my arrow sticking from her chest. She seemed in no apparent discomfort.

It was worse than I had thought! Jehovah God had resurrected the chicken to stand as a witness against me for my sin! There was, I had no doubt, buried somewhere in the Old Testament, a specific law dealing with seven-year-old boys shooting arrows at innocent chickens.

I ran to the house and cowered in the living room, until the sound of tires on gravel told me that my father was home. I watched from the window as he got out of the car, still wearing his hardhat and carrying his black lunch box. He stopped as the old man walked up to the fence. They stood talking, looking at the homemade arrow the old man was holding in his hand.

Hoping for a quick and merciful death, I waited as my father came in and washed up for supper. When nothing was said, I decided I was being allowed a last meal. Daddy said the blessing and began to eat.

The beans and fried potatoes tasted like cardboard as I nibbled small bites. Larry watched from across the table, his appetite unaffected.

"Somebody shot one of Mr. Hall's chickens with an arrow," my father said, sending terror up my spine.

"Did it die?" Momma asked.

"Naw, chickens have thick muscles in their breasts. It was just a homemade arrow. He thinks some kids from over on Mynatt Road did it."

They did not know! I was saved. Hallelujah! Someone else was being blamed for the arrow.

As relief flooded through me like a soothing balm, I vowed to become a Baptist preacher who would spread word of God's mercy across America and to deepest Africa.

"You boys know better than to put metal points on your arrows, don't you?" My father took a bite of beans and cornbread.

Both of us nodded vigorously.

"Good, because it's dangerous. Somebody could get hurt real bad."

Of that I did not have to be warned. I knew someone could be hurt because of the lethal arrows. I even knew who it was. And he definitely did not live over on Mynatt Road.

—17—

Wild Frontier Behind
the House

*A*FTER TWO YEARS, my father gave up on farming his one-and-a-quarter acres on Rifle Range Road. He never said why. More than likely, it had to do with profit margin.

While there, he gave away hundreds of gallons of milk and enough eggs to feed several families breakfast for over a year. He was also out the price of the little barn he built, one pig that died early, seed, feed, fertilizer, and fencing.

So he decided to go into the grocery business at the corner of Virginia Avenue and McSpadden Street, directly across the street from the federally subsidized Western Heights housing project.

"After all," he said to Momma, "Mr. Gentry raised a family with that grocery store."

There were a few things my father did not factor in, however. Mr. Gentry had long ago paid off the property and building, so that when profits began to drop off, he was able to stay above water. Daddy had to take out a mortgage.

The profits had dropped because the neighborhood had changed. In earlier days, when people ran a tab, they paid their bills. That was when the neighborhood was composed of working-class people.

Those days had passed. The working class had moved away, for the most part, to escape the housing project, which ran from Virginia Avenue all the way to Beaumont, where I would be going to school.

That left a world composed of people with nothing but welfare checks, who did their shopping at the big supermarkets where the money stretched farther.

Dozens of them, however, ran up big grocery bills before Daddy found out the true story. They had no money and there was nothing he could do but absorb the loss. This he did by working his eight hours a day as an ironworker, then working until ten at night as a grocer.

My father was not aware that the neighborhood grocery store had all but gone the way of the dinosaur. Those that survived did so by selling fast foods and other specialty items. He got into the business because he remembered only the pleasant neighborhood grocery stores of his youth.

None of this meant anything to me, however. Having just turned eight years old, the only thing that concerned me was the potential for adventure in the new neighborhood. I found that to be plentiful.

"Stay in the back yard," my father admonished. "Watch the smaller kids."

It was about four-thirty in the afternoon, and my aunts and uncles had shown up to help with the moving. At eight years of age, I was the ranking kid of the seven offspring, who ranged down to three years old.

"Hide-and-seek," I yelled. "Not it!"

"Not it!" Dorothy yelled.

And so it went down the line, until my sister, Pat, then the youngest, was the last to call out.

"You're it! Hide your eyes," I said.

"Why am I always *it* first?" she asked, hands on hips.

"Because you were the last one to say 'not it,' " I explained reasonably.

"It was a trick! I wasn't ready."

"You were as ready as anyone else. Do you wanna play or not?"

"All right. But it was a dirty trick."

"Hide your eyes against the house and count to ten," I told her.

"One, three, seven, nine, four . . ." She had not yet learned to count. We all scurried away, looking for hiding places. Some crawled under bushes, some ducked behind an old wooden shed. I decided to find a super hiding place and make everyone hunt for me.

Standing under the branches of a wild cherry tree, I measured the distance to the lowest limb. Jumping, I caught it and began to pull myself up. Honeysuckle vines running along the fence had climbed onto the limb. I was just pulling myself up to one of the heavier branches when the first point of fire caught me behind the ear.

Yellow jackets! They were smaller than bees or hornets, but much more aggressive. I had rubbed up against their nest. Turning loose to slap the insect from behind my ear, I slammed into the ground. The beasts swarmed down before I could recover from being winded.

They nailed me six or eight times as I half-ran, half-stumbled away, screaming bloody murder. The other children ran out of hiding to watch as I skipped and whirled across the back yard, slapping at my persistent tormentors.

"How do you always manage to hurt yourself?" Daddy asked as Momma picked out the stingers with tweezers and dabbed on baking soda.

Sniffling, I merely shrugged. For an hour I was made to sit and be watched for signs of allergic reaction, until the adults were certain I was not going to die. By that time, food had been brought.

Everyone put away sandwiches, potato chips, and soft

drinks, as they carried in and assembled beds and other fur-
niture. It was dusk dark when I got back outside.

"Wild horses," I yelled. "I'm a black stallion with a white
mane and tail."

"Palomino," Dorothy called out. "I'm a palomino mare."

"White stallion," Larry yelled.

So it went, on down the line until, once again, Pat the
youngest was left.

"I wanna be a white horse," she said.

"I'm already a white horse," Larry, then five, said. "You
can't have but one white horse in a herd. They'd kill each
other. You be a pinto."

"What's a pinto?" she asked suspiciously.

"It's a white horse with spots . . . like Tonto's horse. You
know, the Lone Ranger's faithful companion."

"I don't wanna be a pinto. I wanna be white," she stubbornly insisted.

"Do you wanna play or not?" I demanded.

"All right, but it's a dirty trick," Pat said.

For the next thirty minutes or so, we roamed the plains,
neighing, whinnying, pawing the ground, and avoiding horse
catchers. Then I was challenged.

"It's my turn to be the leader," the palomino mare said.

"No, it's not. Mares can't be in charge. It's *always* a stallion."

"If I can't take a turn in charge, I'll quit," Dorothy threat-
ened.

"Let's have a horse race to see who's in charge," I craftily
suggested. I knew I could beat her.

"Nope," she said, "you run faster than me."

"I'll give you a head start."

After a moment, she agreed. It took about five minutes to
arrive at a compromise on the amount of head start, and the
actual course. When we were ready, ten feet or so of lead had
been decided on.

"One . . . two . . . three!" Larry piped out.

We loped across the back yard, the palomino mare and the
black stallion, in the gathering dusk. I quickly passed the de-

termined Dorothy and was about to yell over my shoulder, just as I made contact with an old rose trellis.

It was two poles sunk in the ground. Once there had been several wires stretched across it. The roses, however, had long before departed. There was only one wire left stretched between the poles. It was exactly at my neck level.

I hit it, running full speed. It straightened out my entire body, swinging my feet upward like a pendulum. I felt my throat constrict in agony as I went flat on my back.

I attempted to tell everyone I was choking, but only a garbled strangling sound came out. They all stood looking down at me.

"I think he's tryin' to talk," Larry said.

"Yeah, he may be chokin' to death," Dorothy added. I certainly thought I was choking to death.

Rolling over, I got to my feet and ran to the house. Inside, I garbled out a few more unintelligible syllables. I immediately had a lot of adults around me, commenting on the large red welt across my throat. After what seemed an eternity, the temporary paralysis of my vocal cords passed.

"Are you tryin' to kill yourself?" my father asked.

"No," I said hoarsely, swallowing very painfully.

"Go out there and sit down! Tell stories or somethin'. Just don't hurt yourself again!"

I went out, muttering to myself that it had not been my intent to hurt myself in the first place. For a while I complied with instructions to be quiet, then someone suggested kick the can.

For the uninitiated, kick the can is a form of hide-and-seek, but if you can get back home and kick the can before the person who is it does, then you are home free.

Sneaking into the house, I found a tuna can that had been left from the evening meal. Gingerly, I carried it out. It had been opened with a manual can opener and was a mass of jagged edges.

"All right!" I dropped the can. "Not it!"

Strangely enough, my cousin Johnny Ray was last to call out. He, not Pat, was it.

"One, two, three, four . . ." he began.

Having learned my lesson, this time I ran only as far as the corner of the house. Peering around the edge of the building, I waited until Johnny Ray was about twenty feet from the can. Charging out, I made a dash for home.

Turning, he saw me. Both of us were running wide open to kick the can first. It was the speed that did me in. In my haste, I misjudged the distance. My foot came down on the can, sliding right into the jagged top.

With a yelp, I danced away, the jagged can hanging from my foot. When it came loose, I saw blood, black in the gathering darkness, pouring from the ball of my foot. I collapsed and grabbed the wounded member.

"I think he's cut about half of his foot off," Larry said calmly.

"I'd wear him out if he wasn't already hurt," was all my father said, as soon as he saw that the wound was not life-threatening. Today, it would probably have meant stitches, but my mother just bandaged the jagged cut and I was walking around the next day.

"I guess you don't care too much for your new home, do you?" Aunt Reba asked a little while later.

"It's the best place we ever moved to," I replied. "I'm gonna have a lot of fun here."

I was not being facetious. I was eight years old. What is a little pain, compared to a wild frontier behind the house?

—18—

Time in the Fiery Furnace

I WAS ABOUT SEVEN the first time a fire and brimstone sermon actually sank into my childish psyche. I'm sure it wasn't the first such sermon I'd heard at the Third Creek Baptist Church, but it was the first that made any impression on me.

There were two different pastors during the first two years we were there, Reverend Arwood and Reverend Hurst, so I don't remember for certain the name of the clergyman who vividly laid out the scenario of Armageddon for me.

Nothing remains in my mind of the sermon, except the first few minutes when the preacher shouted graphically about the smell of brimstone, which he declared to be another word for sulfur.

It just happened that I was familiar with the smell of sulfur.

Two blocks from my grandparents' house on Tennessee Avenue in the Lonsdale community was a chemical plant, called Southern Extract, I think, but referred to by neighborhood children as the "acid factory." The plant either extracted sulfur from raw materials or used it in some other type of process. I had seen piles of the yellow stuff by the railroad tracks at the plant ever since I could remember.

A heavy sulfuric odor hung heavily in the air most of the time. After the first few minutes in the neighborhood, it was like living near an airport or railroad tracks; you didn't notice anything out of the ordinary until you left and came back.

The preacher enthusiastically explained, in no uncertain terms, that burning sulfur and red-hot stones would one day fall out of the sky without warning, accompanied by earthquakes, signaling the beginning of the final battle and preceding Judgment Day.

I'm sure he went on to discuss the fine points, such as whether Jesus would reign a thousand years on earth or take all believers directly to heaven. We finally left Third Creek because my father's interpretation (he didn't believe Jesus would ever set foot on this earth again but would catch us all up in the air) differed from the pastor's, but I don't remember that part.

I never did get past the first two points: (1) The end would come suddenly, at any moment, like a thief in the night, and (2) burning sulfuric rock would fall out of the sky and ignite everything, making the whole world smell just like Lonsdale for whatever time remained.

When I left church that day, I was one frightened little boy. In the months that followed, if I tried to talk to either of my parents about it, they would tell me not to worry because children were all automatically going to heaven, unless, of course, they'd reached "the age of accountability," which in Baptist doctrine means the time when a child consciously becomes a *real* sinner.

In light of that information, I couldn't for the life of me understand why God couldn't have devised a plan to let the righteous and innocent skip the fire and brimstone altogether.

My attempts to alleviate my terror by sharing my fears with cousins and close friends also proved futile. I was usually able to lead my peers in whatever direction I desired, but for some reason the concept of the end of time seemed beyond their ability to grasp. Eventually I stopped trying to share my fears and suffered in silence.

The terror wasn't at the surface of my mind all the time, of course, but it was never buried very deep. Fear would wash over me for no apparent reason as I sat in school or played in my bedroom, and I would frantically look out the window at the clouds to see if the heavenly hosts were gathering to smite Lucifer and his angels, thereby burning up the only world I knew.

A year passed, during which I prayed childish prayers, asking for just *one more* holiday or weekend before Armageddon. Then, like a bolt of lightning, I was hit by another terror that pushed Armageddon completely out of my mind.

The second terror started with a thunderstorm.

Until that night, around my eighth birthday, thunderstorms had held no terror for me. It was an attitude I had absorbed from my father, who, if he ever feared anything except the judgment of God, I never knew it.

When we lived in South Carolina, my mother had spent a lot of time listening to the radio and watching the flat horizon for tornadoes, certain that living in a flimsy trailer, especially in a flat place like South Carolina, might very nearly be classified as tempting God.

Born and raised among the ridges and mountains of East Tennessee, she was never comfortable anywhere else. I knew she was nervous, but my father's calm attitude negated whatever fear she might have passed along to me.

One Friday, she had been particularly frightened because the forecasters were predicting tornadoes in nearby Augusta, Georgia, where we did our weekly grocery shopping. That evening Daddy came home, ate his dinner, then asked Momma if she had her shopping list ready. She told him that the forecasters were predicting tornadoes and she wanted to wait until the next day, but to no avail.

A few minutes later, we were on our way to Augusta.

Though my mother seldom argued once my father had spoken, that day she had blurted out angrily, "What are we going to do if a tornado hits Augusta while we're there?"

"We'll be in trouble," Daddy replied, "but if it misses Augusta and hits Aiken while we're gone, we'll be glad we left. You can't hide from storms," he told her. That was his lifelong philosophy.

So the increasingly loud thunder caused no apprehension that Friday night while we were gathered at my grandparents' house on Tennessee Avenue, along with most of my mother's immediate family. That house was often full of family. In fact, the living room, which was separated from the rest of the house by double glass doors, was very often home for whatever aunts and uncles were having financial problems at the time.

The television was turned off, of course, because it was considered gospel truth, at least among my mother's people, that if lightning "ran in on the television" it might blow up, killing everyone in the house, maybe in the entire block. You just couldn't trust those new-fangled devices like televisions and refrigerators.

It was apparently a pretty ferocious storm. The other children in the house were playing elsewhere, while I had sneaked into Uncle A.C.'s bedroom and gotten into his stack of detective magazines. I was, of course, strictly forbidden access to them, which made them all the more tempting.

I was thumbing rapidly through the garish pages of scantily clad women when lightning apparently struck a nearby transformer, knocking out the lights.

There was a sudden silence in the house, as everyone stopped talking. An instant later, sirens began to go off. I know now that the sirens were part of the civil defense warning system at a fire station a few blocks away. That night they had absolutely no significance for my eight-year-old mind.

When the lights came back on a couple of minutes later, Aunt Coba rushed into the bedroom, turned on A.C.'s radio, and frantically twisted through the stations until she heard someone talking.

"There's nothing on the radio about it," she yelled into the next room, sounding relieved. "It must be a false alarm."

I had no idea what "it" meant, but she hadn't noticed that I had a detective magazine in my hand, so I slipped out of the room, happy that I had not been caught with the contraband on my person.

The importance of what had happened would be revealed by accident when my father took my brother and me to get our weekly haircut the next day.

Cooper and Baldwin's Barbershop was a regular part of my life for more than forty years. I had my first haircut there and my son also had his first haircut there.

Clyde Cooper and Howard Baldwin were fixtures on Tennessee Avenue in the Lonsdale community. One was a Democrat, the other a Republican. One a Baptist, the other was a Methodist. But they spent more than forty years peacefully standing side by side in a two-man shop. If they argued, the customers never knew about it.

Barbershops were always crowded in that era of almost universally short haircuts for men, a decade before the Beatles invaded America, putting many barbers out of business and changing others into stylists. Clyde Cooper and Howard Baldwin remained *barbers* for their entire careers, however.

We sat back to wait, as usual, in the plastic and chrome chairs. When my father fell into conversation with the man next to him, my ears perked up as they began to discuss the previous evening.

"Well, were you here when the sirens went off last night?" the man asked.

"Yeah, I was at my in-laws down at the end of the line," Daddy answered.

"It's an awful thing," the man said. "It reminds me of the air raids in England when I was stationed there during the war."

Air raids? Suddenly I was all ears. What did air raids have to do with a thunderstorm in Lonsdale, a decaying suburb of Knoxville, Tennessee?

"Yeah," my father countered. "It reminded me of when I was on Iwo Jima, just before the war ended. An ol' boy from Arkansas came to my tent and asked me if I knew where Oak Ridge, Tennessee, was. He told me that they had built an atomic bomb at Oak Ridge, no bigger than a football, and that they had blown up a whole Japanese city with it."

"Well, it was a little bigger than *that*," the man said, "but I guess the new bombs that us and the Russians are buildin' may be big enough to just about burn up everything if they all go off at once."

Bombs? Burn up everything?

"Yeah," Daddy told him, "I'm afraid the sirens will be for real one night and when the missiles and bombs stop fallin', the world won't be worth livin' in anymore."

"I'll always keep enough bullets for me and my wife and kids," the man told my father, "just in case."

Missiles! Bombs! Air raid sirens! Bullets for the wife and children! Suddenly the little government pamphlets I had carried home from school, the ones showing horrified children running away as a mushroom cloud rose behind them, made sense.

The talk of drills and bomb shelters that I had heard about, but which held no real significance for me, clicked together in my brain. *They weren't talking about bombs in some faraway place like Europe; they were talking about bombs that could reach Knoxville, Tennessee!*

I began to tremble inwardly. Why had no one told me?

"Won't be much warnin'," somebody down the row said. "Once them sirens go off, missiles will probably hit around here in ten or fifteen minutes. You *know* the Russians will aim for Oak Ridge, and one bomb destroys twenty square miles at a time." (I don't know where he had acquired his data, but nobody disputed it.)

Everyone concurred and nobody noticed that a small boy had gone pale as he absorbed the doomsday talk. It was almost too much to bear. My fear of Judgment Day had been a waking nightmare, but at least people wouldn't be shooting their children on Judgment Day!

When the fire and brimstone ended, we'd all go to heaven afterward, give or take a thousand years, depending on whom you listened to. The atomic bombs, however, apparently cut no slack for the righteous or the innocent.

From that moment onward, my existence was overshadowed by the horror of nuclear weapons and ballistic missiles. I read everything I could get my hands on about the subject—newspaper stories, magazine articles, and government pamphlets.

The fear of Armageddon was pushed aside, and thunderstorms, which had never bothered me before, became things of terror because they might once again set off the horrible sirens that would precede doomsday.

Sirens themselves became a thing of terror, second only to the alert tone sounded on radio and television when there was a test of the emergency broadcasting system.

The fear of sirens I eventually overcame because I had to in order to become first an ambulance driver, then a cop. The alert tone, whenever and wherever I hear it, still strikes terror in my soul until it stops and regular programming resumes.

I know that the bombs remain out there. The Russians and God knows who else have them.

It has always been my suspicion that I wasn't alone in my childhood terror. In fact, I think the fear of young people like me, growing up as we did with no assurance that the world would even be here tomorrow, did things to us that we didn't even realize.

I know it made me hurry, left me feeling that I would never live long enough to do the things I wanted to do.

Who can really say what shapes an individual human life or an entire generation? Personally, I think the fear of nuclear war instilled in me and my peers a sense of urgency that made the world ripe for the many changes in our lifetime, some good, some bad.

That's only my opinion, however, much of it colored by childhood terror. Sometimes I wonder if I would have been a different person if my parents had been of the modern variety—like me—who work at removing all fears from the lives of their children by putting them in therapy at the first sign of trouble. What if it turns out that only neurotics can write and paint?

I wouldn't want to find out. I don't think I'd really change anything, even if I could. In his song, "One Less Set of Footsteps," Jim Croce said, "After all, it's what we've done that makes us what we are."

I think he was right. My fears were torturous for the child that I was, but you get the purest metal from the hottest fire. And you can't get much hotter than brimstone and atomic bombs.

—19—

The Saga of the Yellow Raincoat

*T*HAT I WAS AN OUTSIDER who read books did not help matters at all. A yellow raincoat, however, caused one of the most serious conflicts in my young life. It was an important conflict that left me despising bullies and people who run in gangs. As a police officer in later years, I put the spiritual counterparts of those bullies in jail a thousand times.

"It's rainin'," my mother said one morning. "You'll need your raincoat today."

"All right." I put down the book I was reading, a biography of Kit Carson. The wonders of library books had just been introduced to me in my third-grade classroom. I had never known there were so many books in the world.

The first time I went to the library at Beaumont Elementary I was only allowed two books: a biography of Daniel Boone and a book about dinosaurs.

Two days later, I sneaked back to the library, though third graders only went officially every two weeks. There I entered into a conspiracy with the librarian, who let me take all the books I could carry as long as I came in early in the morning, before school started. That woman was a saint, but I cannot remember her name. She saw a hunger for knowledge in a little boy and fed him.

Through her kindness, I learned about such heroic figures as Daniel Boone, Kit Carson, Wild Bill Hickok, Jedediah Smith, and Sam Houston. It was while reading those books that I determined one day to write books of my own.

That morning I slipped on the yellow raincoat and popped the round, floppy hat on my head. Checking to see if I had my lunch money, my mother put me out the door. Normally I would have walked slowly, reading all the way to school. Because of the rain, though, I put the precious book under my coat and hurried on.

To a little boy, the distance to the school seemed enormous. In actuality, it was about six blocks. Those six blocks took me through the Western Heights housing project, which started just across the street from where my father was struggling to run a grocery store, while still working a full-time job.

A branded man already because I wore glasses and was considered wealthy (anyone whose parents had a store full of candy and soft drinks *had* to be wealthy), I had no idea that the mere possession of a raincoat was about to be perceived as a gross insult by one of my close neighbors.

"Only sissies and mama's boys wear raincoats."

The boy had stepped from a yard along the way and was blocking my path, an unexplained expression of outrage on his face. Like me, he was an eight-year-old third grader.

Earl Gordon was a grubby child, with ground-in dirt around his knuckles, fingernails, and neck. Shabbily dressed, hair always unkempt, he stood before me, fists balled belligerently.

"What?" I asked, startled from my normal state of daydreaming about literary heroes.

"I said, only sissies and mama's boys wear raincoats," he repeated.

As a graduate of the Roman's Trailer Park, I was no

stranger to violence. This was a new lesson coming at me, however. In the trailer park, with its melting pot of people from around the country, they were nonetheless working people, with hope of a better tomorrow, a code of honor, and a fierce determination to be independent.

The housing project was filled with people, most of whom had no hope. Broken, crippled men, trying to raise children on welfare, mixed with the lazy and the trifling, unwilling to work, and women with houses full of children, abandoned by the men in their lives. It was a grinding cycle of poverty that bred a hatred of the world outside, which was passed on to the children.

"I'm not botherin' you," I warned him, "so you'd better get outta my way."

"Oh yeah? What if I don't?" Earl Gordon pushed me backward.

Without further discussion, I plowed into him, fists flailing. In a moment I had him on the ground, rubbing his face into the wet grass beside the sidewalk.

"Say 'nuff," I hissed, holding him by the ear and hair.

"'Nuff," Earl sobbed in frustrated rage.

Watching him run down the block toward school a moment later, I retrieved my rain hat and book and went on to school.

Engrossed in the book I was reading as I walked home, I did not see Earl and the other boys until it was too late. They had me surrounded before I could practice discretion, which even then I knew to be the better part of valor.

"This the snotface that hit'cha from behind?" The speaker was a big boy of eleven or twelve. I recognized him as Earl's brother, Carl. The other four I knew to be members of the notorious Allen family (a fictitious name). There were about ten Allen children. It was said that they all had different fathers.

"That's him," Earl said, wiping his runny nose with the back of his hand.

"I whipped him fair and square. And he started it," I

replied. The circle tightened around me and my heart was thumping. I knew there was not going to be a happy ending.

"Are you callin' my brother a liar?" Carl stepped in closer, looking down at me. Even at that early age, his front teeth were decaying and stained brown by tobacco.

"If he says I hit him from behind, it's a lie."

"Oh yeah?" He slapped the precious book from my hand.

With rage and indignation coursing through me, I threw a straight punch aimed for his nose, but hit his lip, cutting it. There was a momentary surge of triumph. Even if they killed me, I had bloodied my enemy—a bigger and stronger enemy.

Then they were all over me.

Understand this, ghetto and slum kids do not engage in the same type of warfare as middle-class children. There is no grappling and wrestling. It is carried out with the same malice, skill, and violence as among grown street fighters. Even at eight, I knew this.

They dragged me to the ground and held me. One of the Allens, a boy of perhaps ten, kicked me in the face. He was wearing white lace-up suede shoes, with pink rubber soles. I caught him around the leg as he tried to withdraw and pulled myself up.

"Your mother's a whore!" I screamed, coming down on top of him. What a whore was, I had no idea—only that it was a bad name, calculated to damage the Allens worse than physical pain.

Looking back, it seems that the beating went on forever. In truth, it probably lasted a good ten minutes—a long time for a fight in which you are being severely kicked and beaten.

One of the project dwellers who lived at the crest of the hill yelled across the street to my parents at the store and told them what was going on.

The boys scattered as my father waded in. He picked me up and tried to calm me. I was still kicking and fighting, sobbing in outrage when I realized it was over.

"I ain't cryin'! I made him bleed! I made Carl bleed!" Tears were running down my face, burning into my torn and bleeding lips.

"Who was it?" Daddy asked, checking me over.

"The Allens and Gordons," I choked out.

"Show me where they live," he said grimly.

"Bill," my mother said, "these are some dangerous people. Let's—"

"They don't know the *meanin'* of that word," my father said, "not *yet*," as we rapidly walked in the direction I had pointed, the half-block to the apartments of the Allens and the Gordons.

The doors opened onto the same porch and Daddy banged on both of them at once. The Gordons' door remained closed, but we could see a man peeking out from the window.

"Come out here, Gordon," my father yelled. "I wanna talk to you about those little cowards you're raisin'." He waited, but there was no response from inside and the curtain quickly closed.

"That's what I thought!" he yelled. "They're a bunch of little cowards because their father's a coward! Boys become what you teach 'em."

At that moment, Mrs. Allen opened her door fearfully. She was pregnant and holding a small baby.

"Send your husband out here!" my father demanded.

"I'm not married," she stammered.

"Then send out whatever man you're *sleepin'* with now. I wanna talk to *him*."

"He's not here." Her voice trembled before my father's rage.

"Then *listen* to me. If any of your little heathens touch my son again, I'll come back and clean out this whole damned project! Do you understand?"

I gasped aloud. My father had said a curse word. It had not happened since I was five and would not happen again until I was thirteen. He was angry. Mrs. Allen nodded affirmatively.

My father went home and soon became depressed as he always did when he failed God by losing his temper. He took me aside later that evening.

"Son, there's never any excuse for cussin' like I did this afternoon. The thing is settled now. Let's just forget it."

Daddy was wrong, of course. It was far from settled. I, however, made plans. I knew the boys were not afraid of my father, nor were they afraid of their own parents. They would get me again as soon as possible. But I had a plan.

The next two weeks were spent on alternate routes home. I learned back alleys and fences well, dodging the Gordons and Allens until they grew tired of stalking me in a group. It was about two weeks afterward when I caught Earl alone.

He was in an alley in the projects eating a stolen Hershey's candy bar. I knew it was stolen because he never had any money and often bragged about stealing from the grocery store across the street from Beaumont Elementary. As I put down my books, he saw me and raised up to run, panic in his eyes. I blocked the way.

"My brothers'll git you." He sneered defiantly, his eyes casting about for an escape route. There was, however, a fence behind him.

"Your brothers ain't here. I'm gonna whip ya. If your brothers or the Allens bother me again, I'll get even every time—if it takes the rest of my life. Let's go."

I raised my fists and advanced.

Earl was game. I'll give that to him. I was bigger, though, and filled with righteous indignation. In a few minutes I had thrashed him into weeping submission. A boy who has been whipped by a gang has no fear of a lone opponent. Earl sat on the ground sobbing in rage and indignation.

Opening one of my textbooks, I removed an object I had been carrying since the day of the beating. "Put this on." I tossed him the folded yellow rain hat.

"I ain't gonna do it," he sobbed.

"Yeah, you will, or I'll whip you again—and I'll tell the man at the grocery store you've been stealin' candy bars. He'll have you sent to the juvenile."

With tears running down his grimy face, Earl picked up the yellow rain hat and put it on.

"Pick up my books and carry 'em for me." It was the final part of my plan.

In a few minutes we strolled past the point of my earlier beating. The residents came out on the porch to watch Earl carrying my books, wearing the floppy yellow rain hat. Had his older brothers shown up, the thing might have started over. But they didn't.

The spectators knew what had happened. Western Heights housing project, even then, operated under the law of claw and fang.

The saga of the yellow raincoat ended that day. Earl somehow convinced his brothers and the Allens not to bother me again. Had they given me another beating it is possible I might have abandoned my revenge, but I do not think so. In the jungle of childhood bullies, I had fought for my place and won.

There was as much triumph in my life that day as I would ever again experience. It is the small things that shape us.

Things like yellow raincoats and nearsightedness.

— 20 —

The
Merchant's Children

MY FATHER'S GROCERY store sat on the north side of Virginia Avenue, just west of McSpadden Street. The neighborhood was called Beaumont. Beaumont bordered Lonsdale. It was a tossup at that time as to which of them was the roughest neighborhood in Knoxville—the roughest white neighborhood, that is.

Racial segregation was so clearly laid out at the time that black neighborhoods were an alien nation. The races mingled on downtown streets, but otherwise were separate.

Even the federal housing projects were totally segregated. I was fourteen before I knew about segregation as a social order. It worked so efficiently that the question never came up.

"Colored" and white did not mingle. It was a law as immutable as the law of gravity. We lived in different places.

I never questioned why there were separate bathrooms and water fountains. When I found out what segregation really meant at the age of fourteen, the revelation shook me so badly that I have never completely recovered.

The clientele of my father's store, given the location

across the street from a federal housing project and border-
ing the second (or first) toughest white neighborhood in
Knoxville, were not the most prosperous.

Daddy proved to be an easy mark. People ran up bills they
never intended to pay, knowing there was no way anybody
could collect from them. Sometimes he went on giving them
credit, even after he discovered what they were doing to him.
One was an old buddy of his from the Marine Corps.

One afternoon I watched as my father bagged up groceries for Ben, a tall and lanky man with short hair. He always came in and immediately began to talk about boot
camp and when he and Dad had waded ashore at Iwo Jima
together. As they reminisced, he would assemble a pile of
groceries

That day, my father bagged the items and carefully entered the amount in his book. I knew the situation because I
had overheard him telling my mother. I waited until the man
was gone, then turned to him.

"He ain't ever gonna pay you, is he?" I asked, sipping a
Royal Crown Cola with a bag of peanuts poured in it.

"I guess not," Daddy conceded. His ruddy complexion
contrasted with hair already nearly white at the age of
twenty-nine or thirty.

"Then how come you keep lettin' him have groceries?"

"Because some day I'll have to stand before God and I
don't intend to have the Lord say, 'I was hungry and you fed
me not.' Ben will answer for what he steals from me, but I'll
answer to God for little children who might go hungry on
my account. Never forget, son, that we all will answer to
God, sooner or later."

My father's attitude was good Christianity, but bad eco-
nomics, which was one of the reasons the grocery store went
under in a year. He worked at it manfully, though his children did not always make it easy.

There was the watermelon episode, for instance.

Where my father found the truckload of watermelons I do
not know. It wasn't a big truck, but it was a special occasion

for a small grocer. He hired a couple of adolescent loafers to help him and the truck driver unload the round, dark green Florida melons.

I eased around the house followed by my brother and sister to see what all the excitement was about. Not quite nine, I was followed by Larry, five at the time, and Pat, who was three. We were forbidden to be out front without permission. Our domain was a fenced-in back yard, which could only be reached by going through the house. Sometimes, though, if he was busy, Daddy didn't notice.

He and the other three were busily unloading the little truck.

"Wow!" Larry said. "Look at all them watermelons. There must be a zillion."

Without warning, Pat ran toward the back of the truck. Our cover was blown and I was in charge.

"Daddy, can we have a wallermelon?"

He stopped and wiped sweat from his forehead. His only daughter stood waiting, barefoot and clad in cotton panties.

"Sure you can," he said. "Here, David," he hoisted a good-sized melon, "carry this in and have your mother put it in the refrigerator. When it's cold we'll eat it. Come back out and bring your wagon. We've dropped some melons and I want you to take 'em around to the garbage cans."

I struggled in with the melon, then ran to get my red wagon. My brother and sister were already nagging Momma about how long it would be before the melon was cold.

Loading the broken melon fragments into my wagon, I admired the large pyramid that my father had constructed. As I recall, the hand-lettered sign said "Fifty Cents Apiece."

Our garbage cans were discarded fifty-gallon drums, the kind everyone used back then. It took a sturdy man to work garbage trucks in those days. The cans were in the alley, just behind the wire fence enclosing our yard.

Pat and Larry were already in place at the back fence, feet propped up in the mesh, waiting to watch me unload. Like me, Larry was cotton-topped as a kid, but Pat was a brunette with freckles (just like our mother) from infancy.

"Look how red they are inside," Larry said.

"I can smell 'em all the way over here," Pat added. "Uhmmmmm!"

"Ours will be cold in a little while," I stated with the wisdom of the eldest child, while I emptied the broken melons into the garbage can.

"Momma says it may be *hours*," Pat lamented.

"Yeah," Larry joined in. "That's a *long* time."

"Naw," I replied, "it'll be time before you know it."

A few minutes later I parked my wagon outside and slipped into the store. Sometimes, if I sat still, Daddy allowed me to hang around. It was one of the few benefits of being firstborn. I slid behind the counter, to the very back.

From that vantage point I could see the candy. Nothing cost more than a dime. My mouth watered at the very thought of the candy bars—Butterfingers, Mounds, Almond Joys, Baby Ruths, Milky Ways, Three Musketeers, Mars Bars, O. Henrys, Zeros, Hollywoods, Hersheys (plain or nuts)—and other types of candy. The penny and two-for-a-penny candies were legion, a smorgasbord of sugary delights to be agonized over when you had a nickel to spend.

My father went to the drink box and picked up a Coca-Cola and a Royal Crown Cola and opened them. He handed me the RC, signifying that he had seen me come in and that I could stay a while.

"Business has been pretty good today," he said, reaching into the candy case and handing me a Hollywood bar, one of my favorites. "Days like this, I think the store just might make it."

As I bit into the layers of dark chocolate, caramel, and white nougat, the door opened and Lola Varner came in. She was enormous and lived, I knew, over on Vermont Avenue, where I had been born. She always carried her own shopping bag.

I nibbled at my Hollywood bar, trying to make it last as long as possible, as my father totaled up her order and packed it for her. She got to the door and turned.

"By the way, Mister Hunter, did you know your children

were out in the alley eating watermelon from the garbage cans?"

She glanced pointedly at the pyramid of watermelons on the porch, then flounced out.

The look on my father's face was one of acute pain. Because of his childhood poverty, appearances were extremely important to him. I followed him out, leaving my RC and candy bar as he locked the store and walked around the building.

Sure enough, Pat and Larry were both sitting in the alley by the big garbage cans, happily stuffing their faces with warm watermelon, juice running freely down their bare chests and stomachs. The air was filled with wasps and flies, also out for a feast.

They both stood up, dropping their heads as their father approached. It was a crime of major proportions. They had directly disobeyed several orders, the major one being that they were outside the fenced yard without permission. They had climbed the wire fence to avoid detection by Momma, who watched the front exit at all times.

The explosion did not come. Daddy merely pointed toward the house. The procession went slowly to the front door. One crushed father, two subdued children, and one curious elder son. He called my mother to the door and gave the offenders over to her custody.

I followed him in and resumed eating my candy as he waited on customers who had stacked up while we were gone. Finally, caught up, he sat down with his face between his hands.

"The whole neighborhood probably saw my kids eatin' watermelon out of a garbage can—and me with two hundred watermelons on my front porch."

"They couldn't have been there long," I said. "They was in the back yard when I came in."

"Yeah?" Daddy looked hopeful. "Maybe Mrs. Varner was the only one who saw them."

He got up as the door opened. It was an old school chum of his who lived a couple of blocks away.

"Bill, did anybody tell you that your two youngest were out in the alley eatin' out of a garbage can? I just heard somebody talkin' about it down at Minhinnet's Grocery."

My father's final decision to close the grocery store may or may not have been caused by my brother Larry's first venture into capitalism at the age of six. In any event, it definitely did not help the situation.

The entire time he had the grocery store, Dad continued to work as an ironworker. When he was rained out, on weekends, and after work he was in the store, trying to make a profit. Mom kept it open during the day.

I don't think it ever turned a profit, not really. Some days were worse than others, though, as my father tallied the books and found out how far he was in the hole.

One afternoon, Larry, then a chubby first grader with a front tooth missing, stopped in to visit after school. After the greetings, Dad noticed that Larry was carrying a bag.

"What's in the bag?" he asked.

"Candy," Larry answered, proudly extending the brown paper bag. It was filled with penny candy—Tootsie Rolls, jawbreakers, licorice, lollipops, and similar treats.

"Where did you get the money for this?" Dad was alarmed. He had come to fear that his children would be influenced by their surroundings to enter a life of crime.

"I'm in the bottle business," Larry said. "I sold some old bottles at Minhinnet's Grocery. He gives two cents each for 'em. It's called a 'posit."

"It's called a *deposit*," his father said, looking relieved. "Don't do it anymore, though. I don't want you prowlin' through alleys, lookin' for empty bottles. I give you more candy than you need, anyway."

"I didn't prowl through the alleys," Larry replied proudly.

"Then where did you get the bottles?" Daddy asked, a horrible suspicion dawning on him.

"There's hundreds of 'em stacked on the back porch," Larry innocently said, unaware that his father had just finished the month's bookkeeping in red ink.

"You took *my* bottles and sold them to Minhinnet?"

Larry nodded his head, backing toward the door. He did not know what had happened, but childhood wisdom warned him that an eruption was imminent.

"I have to *pay* for those bottles! They cost *me* two cents deposit. Do you think free things just lay around the house?"

Larry nodded affirmatively.

"Well, they *don't.* How many bottles have you carried off, anyway?"

Larry answered with a shrug, then darted out.

"He could have at least spent his money here," Dad said in an agonized voice.

Hunter's Grocery closed shortly thereafter and Larry was the only one who cleared a dime from the enterprise.

—21—

Straight from the Devil's Workshop

I DO NOT KNOW exactly how old I was when the ghostly lights first began to appear behind neighboring windows, as people watched television with the lights off. But I do know I was nine before we had a television in our house.

"It's right out of the devil's workshop," Daddy said, "invented to keep people out of church on Sunday night."

It was probably around 1952 when people in our economic stratum first began to acquire the electronic boxes, at least in Knoxville.

Aunt Coba's husband, W. A. Gilreath, bought the first television in the family. He was always an innovator—and not in the least religious.

The first time I ever saw a real television at his house, there was nothing on but the test pattern. That was fairly common then. We all sat in the dark and watched the test pattern, amazed at the wonders of modern technology.

The turning point came a year or so later, when my Grandfather Goin bought a Motorola floor model with a fairly large screen. He wanted it so he could watch Edward R.

Murrow, who had fascinated him over the years as a radio newsman.

As time passed, lots of people began to buy television sets, but there was still no stigma attached if you did not have one. The first real challenge to my father came when Walt Disney presented his series on Davy Crockett. Crockett mania struck the country. Everyone was talking about the frontier hero from Tennessee.

I *had* to see that series or become a social outcast. So I nagged my mother, who nagged my father, who finally took us to my grandparents' house to watch it every Sunday evening until the series was over.

It made a lasting impression. Becoming a Davy Crockett devotee, I ate, drank, and slept Davy Crockett. Our little barn became the Alamo, where countless times my brother and I died trying to repel the evil forces of Santa Anna.

Years later, reading the real history of David Crockett, who was a slick politician, I was devastated that history had dared tamper with Walt Disney's script.

There was another problem caused by the Disney special. We discovered that *Lassie* came on after Disney, and we usually managed to hang around for that show, also. And, of course, if you watched Lassie on Sunday, you couldn't neglect Rin Tin Tin on Friday. It was another burden on my father's shoulders, but he bore up under it.

"Television's just a fad. It'll pass away and people will go back to their radios, where the *real* news is," Daddy said every time he drove to my grandparents' house to watch television.

From the time that Bill Gilreath bought his first Motorola television, Dad held out for about three years.

We were laughing, my brother and I, uproariously, at the *Our Gang Folly* films, being presented new to our generation as *The Little Rascals*.

"It's time for supper."

We looked up to see our father standing at the front door of our next-door neighbor's house. He was still wearing his work clothes. It was the third evening in a row that he had found us there.

"It's almost over," we yelled in chorus. "Let us watch the rest of it."

"*Now*," he said, ending the discussion. We reluctantly followed him home. At the table, it was time for serious discussion.

"We don't have a television because I don't want my kids watchin' it all the time," he told Momma.

"They just watch a *little* every week," she replied, cutting up my sister Pat's pork chop. "I don't see anything wrong with what they watch."

"It's the principle. It doesn't do any good for me to take a stand, if my family won't support me in it."

"I hear Reverend Hurst has bought a television," Momma added, taking a bite of mashed potatoes. "He says if church shows come over the air, television can't be all bad."

Daddy had obviously lost an important ally. He thought highly of Reverend Hurst, who had replaced the pastor who had gone off to preach at a big church that was using the "red-backed Pentecostal hymnal." The red-backed hymnal was causing a division between Baptists in those days.

It had to do with the hotly debated question of whether the millennium (Christ's reign of a thousand years on earth) would come before or after the judgment. My father held that it would be after, while the people who sung from the red-backed hymnal generally believed it would come before.

"Well, I don't have to go along with it, no matter who else does!" Daddy said, though obviously crushed by Reverend Hurst's desertion of principle. There was not much fire left in him on the subject.

"Television! Television!" Larry, then five, yelled, running through the front door, one Saturday afternoon.

"Yeah! Telebision! Telebision!" Pat yelled, mimicking Larry as best she could.

Our father came through the front door, a grim expression on his face. He was carrying a television, but one like we had never seen before. It had a round screen.

It was the only round screen I ever remember seeing. Dad had a talent for bargains that was unique. Television had arrived in Knoxville with the traditional square screen. He had managed to find a virtual antique.

No matter. We had a television at last! All of us danced around in anticipation as it was plugged in, then we watched as the screen began to roll. In the end, we found that the television received only one station and someone had to hold the antenna ("rabbit ears," we called them) at all times. We took turns.

"I got tired of findin' my kids at other people's houses," our father said in his own defense.

Through the remainder of that Saturday afternoon, Daddy watched disdainfully as we sat enraptured, from time to time making comments about wasted time. He was about to be overtaken by fate, however.

For the first time that evening, we heard the theme of *Gunsmoke*. It throbbed through the house, drawing even our father's attention. The unsmiling Matt Dillon strode into our living room. By the time the bad guy bit the dust, Daddy was engrossed. I do not think he ever missed *Gunsmoke* again.

"Maybe there is *some* good in television. It shows that crime never pays," he conceded.

Some time in the next couple of weeks, he came home with a real television. It was not new, because he never bought anything new if he could help it. But it had a square screen, picked up all three channels, and we did not have to hold the antenna to watch it.

Soon, Dad and I were sitting up on Saturday nights, watching the wrestling matches and old movies. His attitude never entirely changed, but he came to appreciate television's good points. *Bonanza* was one of those good points. He sympathized with Ben Cartwright, attempting to raise three sons alone.

Some things outraged him, like the time Lucille Ball, during an episode of *I Love Lucy*, appeared in her slip. It was, my father declared, the "beginning of moral decay in America," proving that television was from the devil's workshop when a married woman walked around, without embarrassment, in her underwear. He wondered aloud why Desi Arnez allowed such a thing.

Had he lived long enough, Dad might have become a crusader against immoral programs. He died, though, in 1968, missing the advent of cable and adult movies piped into the house.

As for me, television was a turning point. It was a fusion of imagination and technology. It inspired my imagination to new heights. It opened new horizons.

The trend today is to discourage children from television, to shoo them outside for fresh air and exercise because television is "not good for them."

I don't necessarily hold with that theory. Of course, I never understood the benefits of chasing any kind of ball around a field and never understood how sports was supposed to build more character than episodes of *Superman*, where the good guys always won.

In fact, if I had become enthralled with sports, I doubt that I ever would have become a serious writer.

There is a lot to be said for watching too much television, even if it is made in the devil's workshop.

—22—

A House Built
of Scrap

*T*HIS IS NO PLACE to raise kids. I'm gonna build a new house on Rifle Range Road and move back to the country," my father declared. "I don't know what was on my mind when I bought the grocery store in *this* neighborhood."

"You just moved away from Rifle Range Road a couple of years ago," W. A. Gilreath, my Aunt Coba's husband, said. He was a small man, always cynical, who could sell icemakers to Eskimos if he set his mind to it.

He could never sway my father, though. He had advised against the ill-fated grocery store venture, but Dad seldom listened to anyone—unless they said what he wanted to hear. The grocery store had gone under and my father had promptly opened a small grill, which also went under.

He probably could have made a success of any of his many ventures, if he had turned loose of his union ironworker's card. It was his security, though, and he kept it up until he died.

"I know, and it was a *mistake*. Besides, I need more room. Pat's almost five now and she still sleeps in the same room as the boys."

"Why don't you just *buy* a house?" W.A. asked reasonably. Always curious, I was hanging around while my cousins played in the back yard with my brother and sister.

"Because I've figured out a way to build it for about half of what I'd pay for one."

"How?"

"I'm gonna build it from scrap."

"Well," W.A. replied with a shake of his head, "I think you're bitin' off more than you can chew. Good luck, though."

The venture had begun as we were out for a Sunday afternoon drive and a trip to Wallace's ice cream parlor on Clinton Highway. It was a ritual. Wallace's served homemade peach, strawberry, chocolate, and vanilla. I have never eaten such ice cream since, or so it seems, filtered through the memory of childhood.

We drove down Rifle Range Road that afternoon and Daddy waxed nostalgic about his little farm, commenting that the new owner was not keeping up the barn. He had already forgotten his financial disaster. About a quarter of a mile east of our little farm he saw a For Sale sign and stopped.

Under a rush of inspiration, he wrote down, then later called the telephone number on the hand-lettered sign. Two days later, he had made a down payment on a couple of acres of woodland, which gave him a new payment at one of the hated finance companies, which he always called "the bloodsuckers."

Poor people with little collateral had (and I'm sure still do) trouble borrowing from banks. My father owed finance companies most of his life.

With a borrowed axe and saw, he descended on the property that weekend. In a few days, he had cleared enough trees and bushes to start digging the footers. Having no idea how to begin, he looked up a carpenter on the job where both of them were working. The carpenter told him how to lay it out.

By hand, he dug and poured the concrete footers, a big undertaking, usually done (even in 1956) by machinery. When it was time to build the foundation, for once Dad took advice. The carpenter assured him that he needed a block mason to lay the foundation. That was his last compromise.

We got out of the 1939 Ford truck and walked up to the edge of the lot, where an old mansion was being torn down. In a few minutes, a fat man in a plaid jacket with a big cigar in his mouth strolled over. He was obviously a prosperous man—and in charge.

"What kin I do for ya, neighbor?" he asked, removing the cigar.

"I wanted to check on the price of that hardwood you've ripped out," Daddy answered.

"Whatta ya want with it? Nobody even uses that kind of flooring anymore. It's too expensive to make."

"We're buildin' a house."

"Who is *we?*" the man wanted to know, as he puffed away.

"Me and my boy, here."

"Just the two of ya, huh? You ever built a house before?"

"Nope, but the foundation's ready."

"What makes you think you kin do it?" the man asked curiously.

"Because anything that anybody else can do a *lot* of, I can do a little of," my father answered.

"Take the hardwood," the man said. "Do you have plumbing?"

"No. I'm just gettin' started."

"We'll be here a week. You carry off everything you can before then, because this lot has to be vacant by Friday," the man said.

"I don't have that kind of money," my father replied. "I just wanted the hardwood."

"Mister, I grew up in that house. I didn't wanna tear it down. My family got a court order to make me sell the property. I'd rather have a *real* family walking on that hardwood and usin' whatever else they can, than to get a few dollars for it. Take it—no charge. A man who builds a house with his own hands deserves a little help."

Slowly the house went up. I pulled nails from used lumber and straightened them for later use. With borrowed tools and tools bought at junk stores, Dad sawed and hammered. Each new task was a new challenge.

When it was time for plumbing, he found a pipe fitter, who loaned him tools and books; an electrician did the same when wiring was needed. I crawled under the house, pushing the electrical wiring up through the holes until we were finished.

We were not alone after a few months. Neighbors began to drop by. When a tool was needed, it appeared. When there was heavy lifting, help was recruited. Everyone was curious about the man building a house from scrap, assisted by his nine-year-old son.

The fireplace drew a lot of attention. Fireplaces were out of style at the time, but Dad wanted one. Searching for a bargain, he found a stack of specialty bricks. They had been declared excess, probably because of the color, a pale green. Who wanted green stone in a day of white houses and red brick?

My father found a book and built the fireplace and chimney. By that time, the house was enclosed, though the outside was still covered only with tar-paper—a minor detail, Dad decided. He sold the grocery store building and we moved in.

There was still a lot of work to be done. Nothing was painted inside. The lot had not been graded. It was warm and dry, though, and we had built it with our own sweat and muscle. There were three bedrooms, a bathroom, a spacious living room, and a kitchen; it was the best house we had ever owned.

"You can't paint a house *yellow*," admonished Mr. Gardner, the elderly neighbor from across the street.

"Why not?" Dad asked, already stirring the pale yellow paint.

"Because *nobody* paints a house yellow around here. That's why."

"*I'm* painting a house yellow."

"Why? Why yellow?"

"It was on sale," my father replied, "half price. And I *like* the way it looks."

"What if purple had been on sale? Would you have painted your house purple?"

"I might have." He dipped his stick in, checking the consistency.

"What color are you going to trim it, *black*?" Mr. Gardner asked.

"No. The foundation and shutters will be green."

"*Green*? Everybody's gonna laugh at you. A green and yellow house?"

"They all laughed when I said I was gonna build it in the first place. Now it's built. Let 'em laugh," my father said.

Mr. Gardner was wrong. Nobody laughed at the finished product. That house was absolutely striking. The green paint (also bought on sale, of course) complemented the pale green chimney perfectly. For a long time it was the most beautiful house on Rifle Range Road.

Somewhere my father had found a load of large, round river rock, which he painted white and used to line the driveway. Driving down the highway another day, he had spotted a load of junk on an old truck. Piled on top were two old wooden wagon wheels. He flagged the truck down and bought the wheels.

Painted white, standing at the entrance to the driveway, they triggered the idea for the white wooden fence across the front.

The house of scrap slowly became a neighborhood show place.

"Your Grandfather Hunter built that house," I told my son, Paris, as we leisurely drove by one day. "He built it with his own hands and I helped, over thirty years ago. Look at it. The chimney still works after all these years."

"He died before I was born, didn't he?" At six, Paris was still a little vague on time.

"Yeah, he died a young man," I answered, "but he accomplished a lot. He was a mover and a shaker."

"Did ya love yer dad?" my son asked, staring directly at me.

"Yes, I did, but we didn't get along when I got older. I don't think he ever knew I loved him." Tears began to run down my face, quite unexpectedly.

Among my personal papers is a Father's Day card I bought for my father in his forty-first year. It told him how much I loved him. He never saw it, though. A stiff-necked and stubborn bunch, we Hunters are not good at showing affection. When it came right down to it, I was not able to express such a naked emotion.

He was dead before Father's Day of his forty-second year.

"Were you a man when yer father died?"

"I thought I was, son. I was twenty. Some people take a longer time to become men than others. My father did it early; I guess I was thirty before I finally made it."

"I hope I make it early," Paris said.

"So do I, son. And I hope you're like your Grandfather Hunter. He built a house from scrap. He believed that if anyone else could do a lot of a thing, he could do a little. That's a pretty good way to take on life."

—23—

God Give Me Patience and I Want It Now!

My FATHER'S LIFE was a quest for serenity. He never achieved it. Faith he had in abundance, but serenity eluded him. In truth, it was remarkable that he kept the better of his temper *most* of the time.

Rage was in the genes and in his childhood environment. The Scottish-descended Hunters were every bit as volatile as the French-Canadian Berlands. Both sides produced short, stocky people who talked with their hands, jittery people not given to serenity.

It was a law in my father's canon of ethics that family disputes should be settled away from prying eyes. He never got over watching his family entertain the neighbors with outdoor brawls. At our house, you took family problems inside. Family business was family business.

His disputes with inanimate objects were another matter. On occasion, the neighbors, or anyone else in the vicinity, would be granted glimpses of the Hunter/Berland temper in action.

My first vivid memory of such an event had to do with a can opener when I was about ten years old. The offending device was manually operated and mounted on the door facing in our kitchen.

It had been installed by my father, but he never seemed to remember having placed it there. Every time he walked through the door the handle dug into his shoulder. Every time it dug into his shoulder, he said, "I've got to take that down and put it somewhere else."

It was a busy time, though. He was working full-time and operating a business. The encounters went on for months. They ended about six-thirty one morning.

The sound of nails being pulled from the wall awoke me. From my bedroom I could look directly into the kitchen. At first it looked like my father was grappling with a burglar. My heart began to pound. As I became fully awake, though, I saw that he had the long handle of the can opener in both hands.

There were tears in his eyes (because the handle had dug into the soft part of his shoulder for perhaps the thousandth time) as he strove mightily with the offending device. It was securely fastened.

Finally, with a ripping, tearing sound, the door frame— not the can opener—gave way. He hurled it all away from him. The entire construction crashed into the floor, shaking the house.

He stood for a moment, breathing hard, then picked up his black lunch-box and went to work. That evening, he pried the can opener loose and put the door frame back up. The can opener went into a junk drawer.

I was left with a better understanding of my father and life in general, vowing never to irritate him as much as that can opener had. It was not the last memorable outburst of paternal temper to lodge itself in my youthful memory.

We were getting ready to go to Wallace's for ice cream on a typical Sunday. First Sunday school and church, then hamburgers at home, followed by a drive to Wallace's, then a stop at Aunt Coba's and Uncle W.A.'s house.

In the back seat of our maroon and yellow 1953 Packard, my brother and I were getting the guns of our jet fighter lined up, ready for a skirmish with enemy aircraft. The interior of that Packard was huge. The car was my father's pride and joy. He drove Studebakers and Packards most of his life.

Opening the car door, he reached into his right-hand pants pocket for his keys, then quietly stood a moment.

"Let me have your keys," he said to my mother. "I left mine in the house."

"I don't have mine either," she replied.

"*Why not?*" he asked, color creeping into his face.

"I forgot mine too."

Without a word, Dad began to walk around the house. The back door was locked, as was each window. Furthermore, the windows were of a type he had found on sale. They were metal and rolled in and out. I have never seen that type of window anywhere else.

We all watched as he came around the other side, his normally ruddy face flushed darker. He went to the shed where he kept extra tools and walked out with a lug wrench.

Without a word, he knocked out a front window, reached in, and unrolled it. There were any number of less damaging alternatives, but my father loved dramatic endings. He turned and motioned to me. As I approached, he picked me up and lifted me to the window.

"Get my keys from the dresser," he said quietly.

A moment later, I was back at the front door with tidings that I knew would further distress him. "Here are Momma's keys. Yours weren't on the dresser."

He took the keys and we went back to the car. He paused as he was about to get in. Handing my mother her keys, he reached into his *left* front pocket and got out his keys. He stared at them a moment, then got in and started the car without comment.

I glanced at my brother and we both glanced at our

mother, who was staring straight ahead with just a ghost of a smile on her face.

Momma knew when to let sleeping dogs lie.

The sweat poured from my father's face as he pulled and tugged at the tire tool. He had been at it for three hours or more. At a junk yard that morning, he had discovered a treasure. It was an old Buick with four tires in perfect condition. The tires were for his Packard.

Among the heaviest standard American cars ever made, the Packard required tires heavy enough to support a tank. They were huge and extremely expensive when bought new. My father, who rarely bought anything new, had come home smiling, happy with his bargain of four tires.

He could have taken the Packard to a service station where they would have charged him about seventy-five cents each to mount and balance the tires. It would have taken professionals with the proper tools maybe a half-hour. But that was not my father's way.

Under his logic, sweat was cheaper than cash. To pay someone else to mount his tires would have been to give up part of his bargain price.

The first three tires had taken two hours, counting the time to pump them up by hand. He had been at the third tire for an hour. It stubbornly refused to break down. He had tried everything.

The huge tire would not come off the rim; soap and grease had failed; brute strength and a crowbar had not loosened it.

Finally, my father stretched out on the ground next to the tire, took a deep breath, and looked like he was about to cry. That was always a bad sign. I waited for the explosion.

"I *can* get this tire off," he said.

I merely nodded assent. At such times, one kept quiet.

"I *will* get this tire off," he said.

A lesser man might have taken the tire to a service station at that point. I knew my father would not. I watched as he got up, wondering what type of tool he would return with. As well as I knew my father, the axe was still a surprise.

He only had to swing the razor-sharp double-bitted axe twice. It cut right through the tire with no problem at all. He kept on chopping, however, until it was in two parts.

"*See,* a man can do anything he sets his mind to do," my father told me.

Later in the day, he went out and bought a new tire to match the three he had mounted. It was the only way to make the car ride smoothly again.

Those big tires were hard to find. He let the people at the tire shop mount that one. It cost more than the other three put together.

My father's most memorable encounter with an inanimate object occurred shortly afterward, in full view of several neighbors.

He surprised me that spring afternoon by coming home with a brand new lawn mower from Western Auto. We had never had a new lawn mower before. Always my father had bought his mowers at junk stores.

Mowing our relatively small yard was usually an all-day task, most of the day being spent working on the lawn mower. We had several. At any given time, at least one and, sometimes, all of them were down for repairs. All were battered and dented from past owners.

Noting my surprised look, he smiled.

"I've decided not to start this year with an old beat-up lawn mower. They're more aggravation than they're worth. Go get the gas and oil."

Carefully we filled the mower with the correct amount of oil and measured the oil and gas mixture. Dad wiped off a few drops of spilled oil from the brand-new red and white mower, then stepped back.

"Go ahead and start it," he said.

I pulled the crank cord and nothing happened. I pulled harder and still there was only a sputtering sound.

"Here, let me do it," my father said. "You're not pulling hard enough."

After a dozen tugs on the cord, he stopped. I could tell he was losing his patience, but he said nothing. Carefully he removed the air filter and checked it. Using the manual which had come with the mower, he checked the carburetor adjustment screw, then the oil level.

"Must have been a little dirt or something in the fuel line," he said confidently, pulling the crank again.

The lawn mower sputtered. It continued to sputter for the next half-hour as my father's face grew redder and the sweat poured copiously from his brow.

I was not really surprised when he stepped back and kicked the lawn mower, though our neighbors probably were. It was a small mower and the first kick sent it airborne. He was waiting when it landed to deliver the next kick—and the next.

As the mower went airborne for the second time, I saw the problem. The spark plug was not connected. I did not attempt to intervene until my father was finished, however. One does not step into the path of a cyclone.

He was standing over the mower, like a lion over its fallen prey, breathing hard, as I leaned down and attached the wire. The mower started on the first pull, but there was a loud clanging where the outside housing had been kicked in, impeding the blade.

We took it apart and pounded out the dent—then mowed the yard for the first time with the *new* beat-up lawn mower.

Virtues my father had in abundance. Patience was never one of them.

—24—

The Day the Farmer Ran Away

My GRANDMOTHER Hunter was always breaking things—dishes, doors, tables, chairs, and marriages, if she stayed around long enough in one place.

We always called her Mam-maw Hunter, even though she was married at least once after divorcing my grandfather.

She was already in her fifties when I was born, so my physical remembrance of her was fixed at an early age. About five feet tall, she weighed close to two hundred pounds. In her sixties, she could still knock a door loose from the bolt and hinges—and sometimes did.

The doors were usually accidental victims, which just happened to be in her way as she stalked with deliberate, unwavering determination to her destination. She never went anywhere at a leisurely pace. If there happened to be a married couple behind the door, perhaps engaged in romantic affairs, she simply ignored them, picking up whatever item she had left there—unless they had the audacity to say something, as my father did on one occasion.

"You should knock before you come in here. You don't know what we might be doin'."

"Well, *whatever* you're doing, I've seen it before." She retrieved the bag she had been looking for that morning and went on her way.

Most of her violence was unintended, delivered to inanimate objects. Upon emptying a frying pan or other pot at the stove, she would casually turn and toss the skillet or pot across the kitchen to the sink. If there happened to be anything in the sink, it was gone. She would listen to the sound of breaking glass, then shrug and go on.

If a thread was loose in the carpet or dangling from an item of clothing, she would jerk it loose, completely unraveling whatever she had a hold on. If a cabinet door stuck, it was apt to be yanked from the hinges.

God help the child who got something in his eye and fell victim to the white handkerchiefs she used for foreign object removal.

Not all her violence, however, was impersonal. She could, for most of her years, stagger a good man with her right hook and was extremely combative.

There were at least two reasons for her violent temper. First of all, she came from a family of excitable French-Canadians. Her father, Henry Berland, once captured a weasel in his hen house after going out to check on his squawking chickens.

Twenty minutes later, the family found him, still pounding the weasel (which had been reduced to a tattered, furry rag by that time) against the hen-house floor, while screaming, "Kill my chickens again you sonofabitch!"

The second factor that shaped her into a merciless fighter and destroyer of doors was her marriage to my grandfather at the age of thirteen. He was also possessed of a temper that was legendary even among whiskey runners in East Tennessee.

My grandfather was on the run when he drifted into the Kansas wheat fields, looking for work. A short, stocky man who went bald early, he had joined the army to fight the Germans in World War I. Catching the measles, however, he missed shipping out with his buddies. When he learned that the war had ended, he just left, without bothering to consult the U.S. Army. By the time he was tracked down and sent to Fort Leavenworth for desertion, he had a wife and a couple of kids.

When the federal officers went to get him, my grandmother told me, he was involved in an argument with the man next door. Two years later, the afternoon he returned from the federal prison, he encountered the same neighbor on the sidewalk in front of the family house.

"It's good to see you again, Frank," the man said, just before William Franklin Hunter broke his jaw.

After doing his time for desertion, he moved his family back to East Tennessee, where the entire family became infamous in the poor neighborhoods where they took up residence.

Nominally, Grandfather Hunter was a landscaper. Occasionally, however, he would take off for months at a time, working as a whiskey runner in nearby Cocke County. When he was gone, my grandmother, who had started life in a well-to-do family, supported her children by working as a sewing machine operator in Depression-era sweatshops, becoming more bitter and angry with each passing year.

"There was a rocking chair," my father told me once, "that no one ever sat in. My mother kept it to beat against the wall when she was in a rage. Ma and my older brothers and sisters would take turns beating it against the wall as they got ready for work in the mornings."

Mam-maw Hunter remained poor as a church mouse until fate intervened when she was in her late forties. Oil was discovered in the Kansas wheat fields where Henry Berland had farmed. A share of that land went to his youngest daughter, Laura Amanda Hunter.

She promptly moved to Saint Petersburg, Florida, to be around other retired people with money and married her third husband (I think it was only her third), a dignified, retired dairy farmer from Findlay, Ohio, with meticulously combed white hair.

George was in his mid-seventies when he married my grandmother. Apparently it was a whirlwind courtship, because anyone who was around my grandmother very long learned of her destructive tendencies and ungodly temper.

Taking her back to his neat farm in Findlay, Ohio, he introduced her to his steadfast Lutheran neighbors. For the first time in her life, my grandmother had both leisure and a home base. She grew giant prize-winning tomatoes and flowers. She, at least, was satisfied with the arrangement. It was an idyllic marriage—on the surface.

George and my grandmother would make an annual trip to Florida during the winter. All the children liked George, even if he was a "real old" man, whose hands shook when he unwrapped the chocolate-covered cherries he always brought us.

The entire world thought George was a happy man, until the day he tried to run away during one of their stopovers in Knoxville.

"Bill! Bill! He's gone! George is gone!" The early morning calm was shattered by my grandmother's yell as she hurtled down the hall in her ragged nightgown (her gowns were always ragged), bouncing off the walls and nearly knocking the door to my parents' bedroom loose from the hinges.

"Get up!" she screamed from the foot of the bed. "George is gone!" She charged back to her bedroom without waiting for a response.

"What's wrong?" I heard my mother ask sleepily.

"I think the old man's died," my father said with a sigh, putting on his pants.

He walked past my little sister, Pat, who was about five. She had sat up on the couch, where she was sleeping, eyes wide, watching the theatrics. My brother and I were peeking around the corner.

Dad stopped at the bedroom door, looking puzzled at Mam-maw Hunter stuffing things in a bag.

"He's not here?" our father said, expecting a corpse. "George isn't here?"

"That's what I said, you ignoramus. He's gone! Get your

clothes on. We're gonna catch him. You know how slow he drives. He can't have gone far."

"Oh no. I'm not gettin' involved in this."

"We'll catch him, or you'll drive me back to Ohio," grandmother declared.

Without a word, our father went to get dressed. We children continued to watch the show.

Running into the living room with a dress pulled over her head, but not buttoned, she sat down on the couch, picked up one of my sister's shoes, and attempted to put it on. When the shoe, of course, did not fit, she hurled it against the wall.

It bounced back and she repeated the process—hurling it against the wall, picking it up, and throwing it—harder each time, as her rage grew.

Finally Dad ran in and caught the small shoe as it was bouncing back for the eighth or ninth time. "Mother, go into the bedroom and get your shoes on."

We watched her jog back to the bedroom, amazed at what we were seeing. It was a display of the Berland temper (now called the Hunter temper by spouses) such as we would never see again.

As our father pulled away, northbound, my brother and I walked to the kitchen door. All grandmother's clothes were piled in chairs and on the table. I tried to imagine the dignified old man with the white hair and shaking hands, slinking back and forth from his car to the kitchen until he had rid himself of her things.

Even at the tender age of ten, I grasped the desperation that must have driven him that morning. I noted that the mailbox across the street was at a slant. George always backed up his Cadillac until he hit that mailbox. That was how he gauged his distance.

"I'm sorry, Bill," George said as he sat at the kitchen table. They had caught him before he covered twenty miles.

"I understand," my father said. "A man can do some strange things when he's desperate."

Mam-maw Hunter was carrying her things to the car, saying nothing. We all knew, however, what hell he was going to catch when they were alone.

"Bill, I'm not a young man. Your mother grabs me by the collar and puts her fist under my nose. She calls me awful names. She uses language like I've never heard. And she's destroying everything I have."

"George, you don't have to tell me *anything*. I remember. She's always been that way." My father's sympathy was genuine.

"I'm ready to go," grandmother said. "You come and see us when you can, Bill." She acted as if nothing unusual had happened.

From the porch, we watched George back into the mailbox, then straighten up and drive away with Mam-maw by his side.

"Do you think he'll try to leave her somewhere along the road?" Momma asked.

"No. She's broke his spirit," Dad said. "After she decides he's suffered enough, she'll leave. Then she'll come back here. May the Lord have mercy on all of us, when she does." He was not being facetious; he was never facetious about the Lord.

And he was right—but that's another story.

25

The Summer of My Clumsiness

ALL RIGHT, MEN, get ready!"

I raised the green sapling that was serving as a sword. Genghis Khan and his hordes were about to sweep down on a sleepy village to loot and pillage. Part of my men that day were girls. In addition to my brother Larry and sister Pat, there were my cousins Dorothy and Sherry.

Ordinarily, I would have allowed no females in my army, but one can hardly have a "horde" consisting of only two. Billie Denise, the youngest of Coba and W.A.'s kids, had been denied a place because at three she was "too young" (the rest of us ranged from five to ten). As usual, she had stomped away enraged, declaring, "All right, if you won't let me play—I quit!"

"Charge!" I yelled. We swept down on the unsuspecting victims, swords slashing weeds and saplings in our path. As we neared the bottom of the hill my foot caught on a long root dredged up by recent grading. Hurtling full speed, I was lifted high in the air by my own momentum. I crashed hard.

Crack! I heard the bones in my left wrist break, as sharply as if they had been kindling wood.

"It broke!" I yelled. "My arm broke!" I sat up, grasping my left hand in my right. The forearm sagged like a sway-backed horse from just above my wrist, back to the elbow.

"He broke his arm," Dorothy said, stopping to stare curiously. Soon, the others had gathered around.

"That's what you get for not lettin' me play," Billie sneered.

"Look," Pat said, "it's hangin' down in the middle. It looks *awful.*" At five, she had not been taught to speak soothingly to trauma victims.

I suddenly became aware that my parents and W.A. and Coba were standing in the back yard. They had walked out of the house just in time to witness the incident. W.A. had a cup of coffee in his hand. Given a choice, he always drank beer, but at our house it was taboo. You could have my father or beer, but not both at once.

As they rapidly approached, it occurred to me that a ten-year-old who has just broken his arm should be crying. So I immediately began to cry and ran toward the approaching adults, extending my injured appendage.

"I broke my arm!"

"Your arm ain't broke!" My father said. He always held to the doctrine that if you denied an injury it would go away. He had once insisted that I was not *really* hurt, even though I had just hobbled home with a tenpenny nail, board still attached, all the way through my foot.

"*See,*" he said holding my sagging left wrist, "there's nothing wrong with your arm. It ain't broke."

"Sure looks funny," Pat said.

"I think it may really be broke," W.A. said, sipping his coffee.

"Oh, all right! Clean him up and we'll go to the hospital and have it checked," my father said. "But I still don't think it's broke."

"It's fractured in two places," Dad reported three or four hours later when we returned to the house. I was sporting a cast from hand to armpit.

"So it *was* broken," W.A. said.

"No! It's only fractured," my father indignantly replied, as if any idiot would have known the difference between a broken arm and a fractured arm. He never did admit that the arm was broken.

"What did the doctor say?" Momma asked.

"He says for David to take it easy this summer and not to get the cast wet."

"That's too bad," W.A. said. "School's out Monday. It's gonna put a crimp in his summer vacation."

As I showed off my new cast to my brother, sister, and cousins, I made plans for that last day of school. I intended to go out of the fifth grade as a hero—and I did.

On Monday, as I walked around with the clean, white cast in a sling around my neck, I knew there would be absolutely no one to dispute the story I would tell about how I had broken my arm by falling out of a fifty-foot tree while attempting to rescue a kitten.

I would be king for a day. The little boys would admire the stalwart way in which I had demanded that my arm be set without anesthetic and how I had endured the incredible pain; best of all, the little girls would ooh and ah over the imaginary kitten I had rescued.

As it turned out, that was one of my few fantasies that ever went off just as I planned. The teacher even stood me in front of the room and retold my story, leaving out not a single detail of my narrative.

By the time she finished the story, I believed it myself.

"There," Larry said, "you've almost got it!"

It was a week into summer vacation and the long stick in my hand swayed precariously as I attempted to knock down the wasp nest that was taking shape under the eaves of the house. We were strictly forbidden to bother the paper nests, which were found in great abundance, but that never slowed us down.

Hampered by the cast, I moved directly under the nest. A dozen or so wasps were on it, or hovering about.

"You got it!" Larry yelled, running away as fast as he could.

Indeed I had. It dropped directly toward me. Whirling in sheer terror, I tried to flee, but tripped on the pole I was using. The nest bounced off my shoulder as I finally broke loose and fled.

Fifty yards away, I was congratulating myself on having escaped injury. At that exact moment, the stunned wasp which had fallen down *inside* the top of my cast apparently became aware of its plight.

"Help!" I screamed. "There's a wasp in my cast! Get it out!" Larry, always a practical child, decided that there was no use in both of us being stung. He ran *away* from me as I danced, yelled, and slapped ineffectually at the rock-hard cast.

The sting of what we called a paper wasp hurts. A bee sting and a yellow jacket's sting are very unpleasant (I am intimately familiar with both of them), but they cannot compare with the sting of a common paper wasp. Take it from a veteran.

In desperation, I picked up a stick, sat down, and dug the insect out of the top of my cast. It came out in pieces, of course, but the throbbing continued unabated. A few minutes later, Momma dropped crushed ice inside the cast and called the doctor.

He told her to watch for swelling and tell me to take it easy.

Sitting in the front yard a few days later, I was patting my cocker spaniel's head as he contentedly relaxed. He had the sissy name of Ginger because he had been named by Mammaw Hunter who had no great imagination when it came to pet names.

Two beagles from next door meandered over to join in the petting, shaking their heads from side to side in the fawning beagle manner as they approached. Ginger, his head-patting interrupted, growled, but the beagles ignored him. He growled louder as I reached out to pet the two intruders.

"Hush!" I said. "Nobody's botherin' you!"

The cocker spaniel exploded. He had never been really ill-tempered, but neither had he ever been what you would call a sweet dog. In a matter of seconds, he had bitten both the beagles and me. Then, apparently realizing he had committed the most horrible of doggie sins, he slunk away.

The wound, though not serious, was in my upper lip. Momma disinfected the bite wound, hunted up Ginger's vaccination papers, then called the doctor. Ginger was a few weeks overdue for his rabies shots. The pediatrician told her to come in and bring my father.

I remember well the doctor's words as he leaned back against the table.

"Rabies," he said, "is a disease without a cure. We can vaccinate for it, but we can't cure it—not at this time, anyway. I'll let you make a decision based on what I know.

"First of all, the possibility that your dog has rabies is remote. His last vaccination is probably still in effect. But he could have rabies and not show symptoms yet.

"Normally, in these situations, we put the dog up for fourteen days and watch for symptoms. If the dog has rabies, we start the child on the Pasteur series.

"However, since this bite is to the head region, I don't think we can assume that we'd have fourteen days' grace, if the dog is infected. The brain is the target region for the virus.

"Some doctors would disagree with what I'm about to say, but some doctors have never seen a child die with rabies. I have. If this were my own child, I'd start the vaccine today. Remote though the chances of infection are, it's possible."

"Then we'll have to do it," my father said.

"I also have to tell you, Mr. Hunter, these shots are extremely painful, expensive, and there is danger of an extreme allergic reaction to the vaccine."

"But you'd give it to your child under these conditions?"

"Yes."

"Then go ahead and do it."

Years later, confronted with the same situation, I would

understand the agony of that decision my parents had to make. To say that the shots were painful is like saying that the sun is mildly warm. They were agonizing and at that time had to be injected into the walls of the stomach.

That afternoon, after the vaccine was ordered, the nurse opened my shirt and unsnapped my jeans. She tapped on my cast and smiled sympathetically.

"You've had a rough summer."

"Yeah. A wasp got in my cast, too." I told her.

"You know what? I think you'd better learn to take things easy."

"I've learned my lesson," I said.

And I had. It was almost a week before I found out that a boy with only one good arm cannot control a bicycle while riding down the steep side of a high, wooded ridge.

Fortunately, nothing broke that time—only a few bruises and abrasions.

It was the summer of my clumsiness.

—26—

Flying Eagle and the Shetland Stallion

*I*N A FIELD ACROSS the street from our house built of scrap on Rifle Range Road was a pasture of about three acres. The people who owned it often rented it out to other people who had animals, but no place to graze them.

At various times, there were mules, goats, quarter horses, cattle, and Shetland ponies. A local breeder would sometimes use the field as a nuptial suite. He only did that when there were no other stallions in residence. Once he left a happy equine couple there while a mule temporarily grazed between assignments.

He apparently thought that since mules were rendered sterile through castration, they were totally harmless. Any farm boy, though, can tell you that supposedly neutered mules can become quite amorous at times. I guess mules are like the eunuchs who once cared for harems—sometimes, I'm told, in ways that would have shocked their masters.

The mule in this story had a great time. When the breeder found out that the mule not only liked sex, but had also conquered and intimidated the quarter horse stallion, it was too late to try again. The mare was out of season.

The breeder did not learn from the experience. The next time he brought the nuptial couple to the field, a Shetland pony stallion was also in residence. The breeder looked at the pony, which came up only to the stallion's knees, and decided he was no threat, which proved that he knew as little about Shetland ponies as he knew about mules. Shetland ponies are among the most ill-tempered of all God's creatures.

All the neighborhood children learned a few things that week also. We were alerted to action when we heard the quarter horse stallion screaming. A horse screaming makes an awesome sound.

Running across the road for a better view, we found the Shetland pony chasing the quarter horse stallion. He was biting out chunks of hair as they galloped across the pasture. From time to time the pony would catch the horse by the tail, dig in his hooves, and cause the bigger animal to stand up on his hind legs, white-eyed with terror.

The quarter horse stallion was trying to fight back, but the pony was worrying him like a terrier, dodging his kicks with ease. When the stallion stopped for breath, the pony would whirl and kick him in the ribs.

They were doing what stallions do. They were fighting over the only available and willing female. She demurely watched from the sidelines, waiting for the victor to claim her.

After an hour or so, the big quarter horse was standing head down in a far corner of the pasture, totally whipped. For all I know, after his experience with the mule and the Shetland pony, he may well have been useless for breeding.

The Shetland pony stallion pranced across the pasture to claim his prize. He literally danced for the dainty mare, his white mane flying in the wind. She waited, eyes downcast, for her midget hero.

That was when the Shetland pony found that he had a problem. The black mare stood over him, shoulder to head. When he attempted to mount her, his hooves only struck her in the haunches. It was a sad sight. The victor could not claim his spoils, though he tried mightily and loudly.

She even tried to help, but horses are not very flexible in

their sex life. After an hour or so of moaning and groaning, the Shetland stallion beat up the quarter horse again, apparently on general principles.

The frustrated pony repeated the cycle over and over again until the breeder came back a few days later and found his battered prize stallion.

It was during those few days that a kid named Tyson from somewhere in Michigan, acting under the alias of Flying Eagle, decided to capture a pony and ride like his spiritual ancestors across the plains. Flying Eagle knew as little about Shetland ponies as the horse breeder.

"Flying Eagle will capture a horse and ride," Tyson said. "I have spoken."

All of us were wearing bandanna headbands with chicken feathers in them. Our faces were streaked with lipstick in lieu of war paint, and we had towels tucked in our shorts to serve as loin cloths. There were four of us, three neighborhood boys in the ten-year range and Tyson, the Michigander, visiting relatives for the summer.

"Black Bear says that you should leave the horses alone," I warned my fellow warrior. "Man who owns them would be mad if he caught us botherin' 'em." I did not add that none of us knew how to ride a horse.

"Is Black Bear afraid?" Flying Eagle asked in a clipped Michigan accent.

"No," I said, bridling at the upstart new kid, "but we have no rope."

"I kin git some rope . . . I mean, Red Hawk kin find some rope," Johnny Pope interjected.

I glared at him but was backed into a corner.

"Get the rope, Red Hawk," Flying Eagle said. "We will prepare the game while you are gone."

The "game" was canned food filched from our respective homes. We had tuna, sardines, deviled ham, and Vienna sausages, with saltine crackers and cookies for desert. By the time Red Hawk, alias Johnny Pope, returned with a coil of thin hemp rope, we had the cans opened and laid out.

"Flying Eagle will trade a brook trout for buffalo meat," he said, eyeing my Vienna sausages.

"Two brook trout for one piece of buffalo meat," I replied.

Reluctantly, Flying Eagle removed two sardines and handed them to me on a cracker. I handed him a sausage.

"Black Bear is a shrewd trader," he said.

Soon only crumbs and cans remained. Flying Eagle tied a loop in the end of the rope, then made a lasso.

"Let us go capture my mount," he said.

Without further argument, I followed the other three across the road and under the barbed wired fence. We passed the dejected quarter horse stallion as he cropped grass and looked at us without interest. It was easy to see he was in the doldrums.

The Shetland stallion had given up on fulfilling his lust. He was spending all his time making certain that the mare did not get near the quarter horse stallion, as she had often tried to do once it became apparent that the Shetland could not carry out his end of the liaison.

As we approached, the Shetland pony gave us a malevolent glance but went on cropping the grass. The mare did not even look our way.

"One of you lasso the little horse. Flying Eagle will jump on while you hold him."

"Little Turtle will do it." Tony Clevenger took the hemp lasso and approached within eight or ten feet of the pony. Luck was with him. The loop fell around the pony's neck, causing it to instantly become stiff-legged. It began to snort.

"Help me!" Little Turtle said. Red Hawk and I charged in and grabbed the end of the rope, as Flying Eagle circled behind the pony.

The Shetland began to shake its head and bounce around. Without warning, it charged the three of us. Before we could retreat, it snapped at Little Turtle. The air was filled with a blood curdling scream.

"It bit off my hand!" Little Turtle screamed, hurtling across the field. "My hand is gone."

I will say one thing for Flying Eagle, also known as Tyson:

the boy had grit. While the pony was occupied with the rest of us, he jumped on its back and wrapped his fingers in the heavy mane. He held on, even after Little Turtle screamed that his fingers had been bitten off.

Red Hawk and I crawled under the fence, right behind the sobbing Little Turtle.

"I'm a cripple," he wept, holding up the injured hand. It was bruised and scraped, but all of it was still there. We turned our attention back to the drama in the field.

The snorting, grunting pony was whirling like a dervish. Flying Eagle, by that time minus his headband and feathers, was hanging on for dear life, eyes wide in terror.

Across the field, the mare had taken the opportunity to proposition the quarter horse stallion again. The stallion was running away from her, watching the Shetland pony from the corner of his terrified eyes.

Flying Eagle might have stayed on that pony, had it not changed tactics. Suddenly, becoming stock still, it reached back and bit him on the leg. That was too much, even for him. With a scream, he abandoned the pony.

Across the field they ran with the enraged miniature stallion attempting to bite chunks out of the boy.

Flying Eagle slid under the barbed wire fence with an audible sigh of relief. The pony stood on the other side, pawing the ground and snorting for several minutes. Then, as if remembering its priorities, it whirled and headed back to the mare.

Four boys, grateful to be alive and in possession of all their fingers and toes, headed home.

As for myself, I made a vow that day: Never would I deliberately fool around with another animal that outweighed me—especially one that had suffered recent sexual dysfunctions.

27

The Magnificent Magnifying Lens

I KNEW I HAD to have it the moment I first saw it demonstrated. A boy from another sixth-grade class was using it to start a fire at the edge of the playground, behind a tree and out of sight of teachers.

What type of optical instrument it came from, I never knew. It was about two inches across and a quarter-inch or so in depth. It would catch the sunlight and direct it to a brilliant pinpoint. If held on a flammable substance for a few seconds, it would cause smoke to rise slowly, followed by a tongue of flames.

"Where'd you get it?" I asked breathlessly.

"My daddy found it." He directed the point of light to a weed growing by the fence.

"Where'd he get it?"

"I dunno." The weed burst into flame, almost taking my breath away.

"You wanna trade it?" I asked, watching the weed as it was consumed.

"What have you got?" he responded.

Desperately, I went into my jeans pockets, cursing myself for not being better prepared.

"I got the whole Pittsburgh Pirates team." I put down the worn baseball cards. "A real police handcuff key, a lucky four-leaf clover in plastic, and a nickel."

"It ain't enough," he stated.

"It's all I've got with me," I said desperately.

"Can't help it." He stuck the lens in his front pocket. "This here lens is valuable. It's the only one of its kind in the world."

"Will you keep it until tomorrow? I'll bring a bunch of trade stuff tomorrow." My desperation was showing through.

"If I still got it tomorrow, I'll look at yer stuff." He walked away, a polished trader, kicking up red dust.

He had me pegged. Even today I am not much of a trader. If we get a decent deal on a car, my wife has to do the haggling. I want what I want—and I want it now.

The night was spent in torment, filled with fear that the boy would trade the magnificent lens and I would never see it again. The next morning I left home with a brown grocery bag, telling my mother that it was material for a science project.

"I'll trade you the baseball cards, the four-leaf clover, the handcuff key, a nickel, this bag of cat's-eye marvels, a lucky rabbit's foot, and a shark's tooth from Florida."

The boy contemplated the pile of valuables, scratching his head, which was covered with blond stubble. He was a slick trader. It would not surprise me to find out that he grew up to be a used car salesman.

"I can't do it. I only collect Dodger cards. Besides, I got a rabbit's foot and all kinds of marvels."

"You don't have to *collect* Pirate cards. That's the whole team, and those are *cat's eye* marvels. Anyway, that's the only shark tooth in this county—maybe in the whole state."

"I can't do it." He slowly began to walk away. "Unless, maybe, you got somethin' else . . ."

It was time to play my ace in the hole. Slowly my hand

came out of my pocket. Extending it slowly, I held out an old Zippo cigarette lighter. I had found it by the road. It was so old that the chrome finish was worn into the brass. Snap! Sparks flew.

"Does it light?" I knew by his eyes that I had him.

"All it needs is lighter fluid or gas," I told him.

"I'll trade," he said, extending his hand.

"I can't let the Pirate cards *and* the lighter go," I said craftily.

"All right. Everything except the Pirate cards."

We both were happy with the trade. I knew my parents would have taken the lighter anyway as soon as I became careless and let them see it.

I had the magnificent magnifying lens and a thousand schemes to use it.

"What're you doin'?" Larry asked.

"Gettin' ready to attack Planet Earth," I replied.

On the side of the hill at strategic locations were tiny paper bunkers and troops that I had laboriously cut out of newspapers that morning. It had taken me hours to prepare for a battle that would be over in a few minutes. But I knew it would be worth all the trouble.

The logic of small boys is not always the logic of the world. Boys will sometimes spend days constructing a model ship or airplane, then blow it up with fire crackers to watch it sink into a pond.

I was ready.

"Who are you?" Larry (nearly seven) did not doubt my logic at all.

"I'm Captain Lancelot, Space Pirate. Earth has refused to obey my command to surrender. Now they will feel my wrath!"

"Get 'em," Larry said. "They shoulda listened."

At that moment, I sprung the magnificent lens on Larry. Focusing on a lone paper soldier with a pinpoint of light, I held it for a few moments. The paper soldier went up in flames, writhing and twisting.

"Wow! What is that?" Larry asked, running to look at the charred corpse.

"It's a death ray," I replied.

"Where'd it come from?"

"I traded for it."

"I mean, what did it come out of?"

"Dunno. A microscope or a telescope, I guess."

The death ray was focused on a small paper bunker. Smoke began to curl upward. It burst into flames, destroying all within.

"Can I do it?"

"Just once," I said magnanimously, handing him the lens.

In a few minutes, Earth's defenses were all in flames. Presumably, they had learned their lesson.

In the following weeks, I discovered many more wonders.

Insects examined under it turned into multieyed monsters. When held up to the skin, it revealed giant craters with treelike hairs emerging from them.

It was possible, I learned, to burn my name on a piece of wood, given enough patience and sunshine. The lens would also induce toads to perform incredible jumping feats if the beam was directed at their warty rear ends for a few seconds.

The possibilities were endless. I might have explored them all and today still have the magnificent lens in my memorabilia box—had I not taken it back to school.

A freckled boy named Jerry rubbed a hole in his paper, attempting to erase the brown spot I had burned there with my magnificent lens. It was all I could do to keep from giggling.

From my back-row seat near the window, I looked for a new target, with one eye on the teacher's desk. The substitute teacher stared longingly at the door. A male teacher in elementary school was a rarity in those days. He had spent most of the morning with his head on the desk, as if not feeling well. I remember that he was a tall man in his early twenties, with a crewcut, lingering acne, and a yellow knit neck-tie.

My eyes fell on the behind of Kathy Simpson. In truth, they fell there a lot. Kathy was older than the rest of us by perhaps two years. Unlike the other sixth-grade girls, she rounded off in strategic places—particularly her posterior.

That day she was wearing a white skirt, tight and thin enough to reveal the outline of her panties. Kathy stood out from the rest of the sixth-grade girls, whose preferred style was full, fluffy crinolines.

I cautiously directed the pinpoint of light to her rounded bottom and waited. In a moment, she squirmed and turned to look down at the seat behind her, a puzzled expression on her face.

I put the lens out of sight behind a library book until she turned back around.

A moment later she looked startled and jumped up from her seat. "All right, Tommy, you'd better stop that right now!"

"Stop what?" the teacher asked, looking mildly curious.

"Tommy stuck me in the butt with a pin . . . or something," Kathy said. Her face flamed red. A sweet and pretty girl, she was not very bright, which was why she was still in the sixth grade at the age of thirteen.

"I did not!" The guiltless Tommy Widner said. "I don't even have a pin."

"Well, you stuck *something* in me."

Even to the unsophisticated sixth graders of that day, Kathy's statement was uproariously funny. We erupted in laughter.

"That will be enough, ladies and gentlemen," the teacher warned. "Master Widner, you will keep your hands to yourself."

"I didn't do nothin'!" Tommy Widner protested.

"Then don't do what you didn't do again. Both of you settle down. That goes for the rest of the class, also. It's fifteen minutes until lunch. Be quiet!"

Silence prevailed as the young man put his head back down on the desk.

It must have been about ten minutes later (just time enough for the teacher to drift off into a light sleep) when my gaze stopped on his earlobe. It was an interesting earlobe that protruded a great distance from his head. I had not noticed it before. It was red and looked a lot like the wattle that hangs from a rooster's neck.

I meant no real harm, but the temptation was too much. The lens had caused no damage to others. Like Kathy, they would twitch and jump, long before any real pain set in.

My other victims, however, had been awake.

Expertly positioning the lens, I put the pinpoint of light on the back of the teacher's earlobe and waited for him to squirm. Nothing happened. I was about to move the lens. Then the tiny blister appeared. Even from ten feet or so away, I saw it clearly.

"Owww!" He stood up, slapping at his earlobe. A look of rage and confusion on his face, he turned toward the back of the room.

Sitting in horrified silence, my mouth open, I did not even attempt to hide the lens until it was too late. Like a rabbit, hypnotized by fear, I stared at him, unable to believe the magnitude of my transgression.

"Why you little—" he comprehended the scene and started toward me, holding his injured ear. The sound of his voice broke the spell.

Jumping from my seat, I ran to the other side of the room, putting rows of desks between us. My fellow students, totally unaware of what had happened, watched in fascination as he pursued me.

"Don't run from me!" he yelled.

I darted out the door and made for the stairs. When my father said that, I stopped. My father, however, had never been angry enough to kill me. I was convinced that the young man in pursuit intended to do exactly that.

He gained a little as we went down the stairs. His silence was horrible because I knew he was saving his breath for running. Most adults who had pursued me through the years were only good for a short burst of speed. But then, I had never bodily assaulted any of them with a death ray.

I burst out the front door, heading for the road, prepared to run the entire six miles to my house, if necessary. I never made it, though. It had been just my luck to enrage an athlete with legs twice as long as mine. He caught me by the collar and lifted me, legs still pumping, into the air.

"Give it to me, you little bastard!" He was shaking me as he hissed out the words.

Fishing the lens from my pocket, I handed it to him. Still holding me by the collar, he examined it, then leaned back and hurled it across the highway. He had an arm on him that would have made a major league pitcher envious.

"All right, young man, tell me exactly *why* you decided to do that." His voice was still trembling with rage, but he had stopped shaking me. It dawned on me that I might survive after all.

"I . . . I . . ."

"Didn't you realize that you could hurt someone?"

"No sir . . ." I began to sniffle. It worked at home, so it was worth a try. "I didn't . . . (sniff) . . . mean . . . (sniff) . . . any harm. I . . . (sniff) . . . swear it."

"All right, all right," he said. "Calm down. We're going back inside and act like nothing happened. I won't say anything to the principal and you don't say anything to your parents. Deal?"

A *deal*? Something miraculous had happened. The teacher was not going to kill me, the principal was not going to drive me from school in disgrace, and my parents would remain ignorant of my most daring feat ever.

Looking back, of course, I know that even in 1959, when there was still discipline in most schools, teachers were not permitted to hold sixth graders in the air and call them obscene names—even when they deserved it as much as I did. He apparently saw his budding career flashing in front of his eyes if the story came to light.

We both got off easy, each in our own way.

That afternoon I sneaked across the highway and looked for the magnificent magnifying lens, but it was hopeless. It could have landed anywhere among the debris alongside the highway. I like to think that another little boy found it and had as much fun as I did.

Such treasures seldom come to a boy. It had cost me, after all, a nickel, an old Zippo lighter, a bag of cat's-eye marbles, a four-leaf clover, a rabbit's foot, and a shark's tooth from Florida.

I still had my Pittsburgh Pirates cards, though. I was not entirely without means.

— 28 —

Uncle Ray and the Big Boar-Hog

COME ON, DAVID," my father yelled up the hill, "we have to go help Ray."

Without hesitation, I left my brother playing in the dirt on the ridge behind the house. We had just seen a movie called *Thunder Road*, a tale of moonshine runners. We had carved the hill behind the house into a series of roads over which we ran our toy cars, by turns being revenuers and whiskey runners. There was always a fatal crash at the end, just like the one Robert Mitchum's silver screen alter ego had perished in.

"Can I go?" Larry, nearly seven then, asked.

"Not today, son," Dad replied. "You might get hurt."

The warning sent a delicious thrill up my spine. What kind of dangerous mission was afoot, requiring only the adult and nearly adult males (which I considered myself to be at eleven) of the family?

"What are we gonna do?" I asked as he wheeled our old Studebaker out of the driveway.

Just being around Ray West was an adventure in itself most of the time. Married to my mother's youngest sister,

Reba, he was not like most other adults. If he caught you fifty feet up an oak tree, he never told you that you could fall and break your neck.

If no other adult was around, he would let you play with knives, axes, and sickles. When I was eight, he handed me without hesitation a 12-gauge shotgun when I asked to shoot it. He didn't laugh when it knocked me down and bloodied my lip.

All his life he remained a sort of perpetual child himself. He was often mistaken for Jim Nabors of *Gomer Pyle* (there *was* a resemblance). Impulsive, I guess, was the best way to describe Ray. Accident-prone was probably how his insurance company saw him.

Ray was not clumsy, merely preoccupied and given to action without prolonged thought. That may have been why he ended up above Norris Dam, the Tennessee Valley Authority's first Depression-era project, as the locks were being opened. On a rubber raft, he and his friends had somehow failed to notice the sirens' warning that the water level was about to be lowered.

By the time officials saw the raft, Ray and his friends had tied themselves on and were being sucked under and popped out like a cork in the vortex of water, as millions of gallons of river ran through the dam. They were rescued in the nick of time, affecting water levels all the way to Chattanooga.

A sheet-metal worker by trade, Ray was never able to explain how his upper lip became electrically grounded to an air-conditioning duct when he pulled himself up to look over the top. Welding leads are not supposed to create a current in sheet metal—but they did, somehow. Ray, of course, kicked his ladder out from under him, then fell like a rock when he couldn't hold on any longer.

Then there was the matter of how he managed to be run over by his own car during an auto accident. I never did fully grasp that one.

I once watched him painting. Splattering himself, he attempted to wipe the silver paint away with his brush, then appeared puzzled when the stain covered the front of his coveralls.

Whatever Ray had going on that day would be interesting.

"Ray bought a big boar-hog this mornin'. While he was tryin' to unload it, it stepped on his foot and got away. It's loose in the woods up behind the house."

"What's he gonna do with a big boar-hog?" I asked. Naive as I was, I knew you didn't eat boars.

"He's gonna breed 'im to his four sows and raise pigs," Dad replied.

"Just one boar-hog and four sows?"

"That's right. You only need one boar." Seeing my puzzled expression, my father elaborated, but not too much. His one previous attempt at explaining the facts of life had left me confused for a year. He had no scientific vocabulary.

"How many roosters do you keep in a chicken yard?" he asked.

"Just one, but I didn't know it was the same with hogs," I replied.

"Yeah, and the same with cows and sheep and horses."

"Oh."

Ray was limping around, agitated when we got there. Three or four neighbors had gathered to assist. Two of them were carrying lengths of hemp rope with loops in the end. They were looking amused.

"He's up on the top of the ridge," Ray said. "Every time we think we've got him cornered, he runs down another path. The woods are full of dog trails." Actually, the trails were put there by raccoons, foxes, and other woodland animals, but Ray was a city boy born and bred, who had only recently become a country squire.

"What do you want us to do?" my father asked.

"We're gonna surround the ridge and move up from all sides at once," Ray said. "When he comes down a trail, we'll run him back up and herd him over toward the pens. John or Frank will get a rope around his neck and all of us can drag him."

"Can you do it?" Dad asked me.

I nodded confidently. After all, I had been around pigs a lot. Pigs had always been my friends, intelligent, loyal, and friendly.

"Get a big stick," Ray said, "he's mean. If he tries to go around you, whack him on the nose and yell at him."

A few minutes later, I was in place on my assigned trail. It was about two feet wide, closed in by underbrush on each side. I could stand up, but a grown man had to bend over. It was like a tunnel running through the woods. From where I stood, I could see about a hundred feet up the trail.

As usual, I let my imagination have free play. I was a Cherokee warrior, waiting for the beast to be driven to me. It would be man against brute, but my will of iron would prevail against any creature.

Hearing voices coming in my direction, I stepped to the center of the trail, the peeled sapling my father had prepared for me raised like a baseball bat. The boar came around the side of the hill, angrily snorting and slobbering.

My mouth went dry as I got my first look at him. Expecting a friendly, grunting pig, I found myself standing in the path of an angry, four-hundred-pound boar. Saliva was frothing from his mouth and his little eyes were as red as coals. Tusks curled up from his lower jaw, protruding from his mouth.

And I was the only thing standing in his way.

"St . . . stop," I whispered hoarsely.

He didn't even pause.

Trapped as I was by underbrush on both sides, there was only one alternative. Dropping the puny stick, I whirled and ran as fast as my high-topped black tennis shoes would carry me.

A hundred yards down the trail, I emerged from the woods and skidded as I turned left. Looking over my shoulder, a worse terror seized me. The boar had not continued on, but had turned in my direction. His little piggy eyes were fixed on me. I was probably the smallest opponent he had seen all day.

"Look!" one of the men with Ray yelled from up the ridge. "The boy's leadin' him back toward the pen!"

I had no idea where the pen was, but I knew the boar was gaining. Zigzagging through the trees and underbrush, I tried to shake him, certain that I was going to die under his cloven hooves, ripped apart by his monstrous, slobbering tusks.

My legs were giving out as I reached the top of the ridge. I would have screamed, but I had no breath left. Then the nightmare miraculously ended.

"*I got him!*" someone yelled. "Ya'll get over here and help me."

Collapsing, I rolled over to watch. The boar had dug in and was squealing in rage as the man tightened the noose. Minutes later, my father, Ray, and the other men were dragging him to the pen. I lay back, thanking my guardian angel and trying to catch my breath.

We all stood watching the big red boar as he checked out his new pen. He had immediately driven the four sows to the rear of the pen and was grunting his way around the edges of the wooden fence.

"That was quick thinkin', son," said the man who had gotten the loop around the boar's neck. He was tall and thin, wearing bibbed overalls. He stood rolling a homemade cigarette. "If he had got down to the road, we'd have been chasin' him all day."

"Yeah, I know. As soon as I saw that he'd follow me, I headed right up here," I said matter of factly. "I knew he'd never catch me."

My father was watching me, faint amusement around his eyes, but said nothing.

"How come he's not payin' any attention to the sows?" Ray asked.

"Give him time," the tall man said, lighting the cigarette. "He's still a little upset."

"*I've* never been that upset in my life," Ray said. "I just hope I ain't bought a queer hog."

"Come on," Dad said to me. "I've worked up an appetite. I could go for a garlic link sandwich from Dutch's."

It was indeed a special occasion to merit a garlic link sandwich from Dutch's Tavern, which was as close as my father ever got to where beer was served. Dutch's sold hot dogs and sandwiches through a takeout window, so we didn't have to go inside. In the car, on the way home, we would munch the sandwiches, horseradish sauce bringing tears to our eyes.

By the time I told that story a few times, the boar had gained two hundred pounds, had grabbed the stick from my hand and chewed it up, and had only been deterred from slashing me to ribbons with his tusks because I had punched his snout with my fist, causing him incredible pain.

After a while, I almost forgot what really happened.

—29—

The Awful Demise of Timmy Tadpole

*S*TAY TOGETHER, CHILDREN," one of the room mothers said, as the class of twenty-odd sixth graders spread out across the cow pasture, gingerly stepping over "cow-pies."

We were on a "nature walk" field trip. In those days, elementary school children of our economic background did not bus off on trips to other cities. Our field trips were really in a field—one within walking distance of the school.

The field was part of a genuine working farm. There were cattle, a barn, a gurgling stream, and a small pond with scum floating on its green surface. The cows turned curiously as we made our way across the pasture, all of us laughing and talking.

"Children," Teacher said, "this is not a game. This is science class. If you don't settle down, there'll be no more field trips this year."

We were not particularly worried. It was the first field trip of the year and as far as we knew there were no others planned. Everyone had brought a brown bag lunch. To the teacher it may have been a scientific outing, but to her students it was a rare picnic.

"Teacher, Teacher!" Ralph Goode yelled. "I need a bottle to put a specimen in." Ralph was a skinny kid with a gap between his teeth that he could put a small pencil through, famous for his lack of interest in things scholastic.

He was kneeling with his back to us, closely examining something on the ground.

"What is it?" Teacher asked suspiciously.

"Come and look," Ralph replied, "it's very scientific."

Detecting a set-up, we all trooped toward Ralph to see what wonder of science he had found. In a moment, the girls were all saying things like "yuck" and "disgusting," as Ralph smiled a happy gap-toothed smile.

"Ralph—" Teacher stopped abruptly as she saw (and probably smelled) the dead rabbit. "Get away from that thing!"

"I want to study some of the maggots," Ralph said. "I need a specimen bottle."

"There will be no maggots taken back to the classroom. Let's get down to the pond," Teacher said with finality.

"Maggots is scientific, too," Ralph argued.

"*Now*, Ralph," Teacher ordered.

Ralph followed along, mumbling to himself about how the "teacher's pets" could do what they wanted, while he, an outcast because of his independent thinking, was treated like a "mangy dog."

"All right, children," Teacher told us, "everyone get a specimen bottle from one of the room mothers. Let's see how many interesting things we can find today. Don't fall into the pond."

Her words were heeded pretty well. Only three boys fell into the water before the trip was ended, Ralph Goode being one of them.

"Teacher, Teacher!" Sharon White called out. "I've found some frog eggs."

We all trooped to the edge of the pond where Sharon squatted, unladylike. Most of the boys, myself included, ran around to the far side of the small pond, directly opposite Sharon. It was a well-known fact that she wore no panties because of a medical condition. Her revealing pose that day bore out the general consensus that she was not overly modest.

The boys punched and snickered, being more interested in female anatomy than frog eggs.

"Very good, Sharon," Teacher said. "It's a *big* clump of eggs. You were very observant."

Hundreds of round, clear eggs, with black dots in the middle, were suspended in a clear jelly just under the surface of the water.

"Can we put 'em in a jar and watch 'em hatch?" Sharon asked, shifting around a little, causing increased punching and jumping up and down among the boys across from her, as new perspectives opened up.

"I don't see why not," Teacher said. "I think I saw an old aquarium in the storage closet."

"Look, look, the eggs are hatchin' out," Sharon White yelled excitedly one Monday morning.

The entire class moved as one body across the room. It was a fact. The aquarium was filled with tiny tadpoles, swimming happily around.

"Can we feed 'em, Teacher, huh?" someone asked.

"That's what we bought the food for," Teacher replied. She was pleased. Few school science projects ever worked out so well.

"How long will it be before they turn into frogs?" Ralph Goode inquired. It was obvious that he was already thinking of uses for the frogs, dissection perhaps.

"We will observe and see, Ralph," Teacher said. "That's the scientific way." That meant, we all knew, she did not know.

"Will all of 'em grow up?" Sharon White asked.

"Well," Teacher replied, "in the wild, fish would eat them. I suppose most of these will survive to be frogs, though we'll have to put part of them back in the pond when they're bigger. The aquarium is too small for many of them."

Had anyone been watching Ralph Goode's face, they might have seen a thoughtful expression.

We never knew how long the fish was in the tank that next day before we saw it. It had to have been an hour, though, as roll call and the Pledge of Allegiance were over. What kind of fish it was, I do not remember, if I ever knew. It was most certainly some kind of local game fish, four or five inches in length.

It was swimming around, happily gorging itself on tiny tadpoles, when Sharon White discovered it. She considered those tadpoles to be hers, because she had found them.

Her scream was long and piercing. She stood pointing as she screamed, a look of horror on her face. "It's eatin' my tadpoles," she sobbed.

A moment later, Teacher had removed the fish with a small net. She turned to look at us, wrath written on her features.

"Obviously someone has no respect for other people." She was looking right at Ralph Goode, who stared innocently back.

"From here on out, we will all closely watch the tadpoles, so that nothing happens to the remainder of them."

Ralph never did admit to putting the fish into the tadpole tank. He did not deny, however, the rumor that his father had a pond, stocked with small game fish, such as bluegill, bream, and crappies.

The second tadpole disaster struck as Sharon White and another girl were cleaning the tank one morning. It was a laborious process, as the tank had no aeration or filtration system. The tadpoles, a quarter-inch long by then, would be taken out in a small aquarium net and crowded into a fishbowl while the water was changed.

Sharon had inadvertently filled the fishbowl from the hot water tap that day. It was not hot enough to even bother Sharon as she carried the bowl back to the room, but it was much too hot for the tadpoles. She had over half of them netted into the fishbowl before they started to go belly up on her.

She was inconsolable for days. The tadpoles, which had once seemed as innumerable as the sands of the sea, had lots of room to swim around after that.

Then, just days later, a horrible tadpole plague struck. We never knew what caused it. The tadpoles would form little white spots all over their bodies, then die. Every morning we took out the dead ones and watched the numbers dwindle. Changing the water daily did no good. Finally, only one remained of the hundreds.

Timmy Tadpole, as we began to call him, was transferred to the goldfish bowl to facilitate changing the water. Despite the disasters that had destroyed his entire clan, Timmy thrived and did not seem to suffer pangs of loneliness. He ate well from the more than ample supply of tadpole food and grew fat.

"Look!" Sharon White yelled one day. "Timmy has legs growin' from his back part!"

Sure enough, Timmy Tadpole was turning into Timmy Frog. Soon, he also had front legs growing. It looked as if Timmy was going to make it.

"Children," Teacher said, "we must handle Timmy carefully from here on out. Sometimes we have not kept the bowl as clean as we should have. So I am making a list. Each day two of you will be assigned to change Timmy's water. That way, each can make sure that the other makes no mistakes."

The best laid plans of mice and men . . .

"Did ya see Sharon White when she climbed up on the chair to wipe the blackboard?" Ralph Goode asked me.

"Naw, I wasn't lookin.'" It was a bare-faced lie. I had been watching as she stood on the chair, leaning forward to display her hidden treasures to all who would look her way.

"Well, I was lookin'," Ralph said, opening the restroom door, "and I think she wants ever'body to look at her. Joey says he puts his head on the desk and looks back at her, and every time she sees him look, she turns and spreads her legs so he can see ever'thing she's got."

"Put the sink stopper down and turn on the cold water, Ralph." I was carrying the goldfish bowl, in which Timmy Tadpole was happily swimming, kicking his stubby new legs.

"Whatta you think?" Ralph asked, pushing down on the stopper handle and turning on the cold water. "Do ya think she does it on purpose?"

"Maybe," I said, pouring the contents of the goldfish bowl into the sink. Timmy Tadpole had no more than left the bowl, when I saw, to my horror, that Ralph, still lost in reveries of Sharon White's private parts, had not closed the drain stopper completely. There was about a quarter-inch of space. The sink was filling faster than the water could run out, but still draining nonetheless.

Without hesitation, as if he had been planning to make a break for freedom at the first opportunity, Timmy Tadpole shot across the sink, moving directly toward the opening in the drain.

Reaching out, I slammed down the lever and drove the metal stopper home. Unfortunately, Timmy's head was already partly through. He was decapitated with surgical precision, the head going down the drain, the body lying unmoving in the sink.

Both of us stared at the corpse in horror-stricken fascination. It was our day to care for him—and we had killed Timmy Tadpole.

"What'er we gonna do?" Ralph asked breathlessly.

"Maybe we can run down to the pond and catch another tadpole," I suggested, grasping at the proverbial straws.

"Naw," Ralph said, shaking his head with resignation. "We'll just have to go tell Teacher what happened."

Since he had more experience than I did with being in trouble, I followed his lead.

There were tears stinging at my eyes as I went in to face my classmates and teacher. I had killed Timmy Tadpole, had chopped off his head, murdered an innocent frog child.

Teacher, however, knew true remorse when she saw it. There was no lecture on "responsibility" as I had expected. She told us that every creature on earth, Timmy Tadpole included, had to die someday, then sent us to our seats.

I think she was glad it was finally over.

That afternoon, several of us sneaked down to the pond. Placing Timmy Tadpole in a matchbox, we set it on fire and floated it out across scummy green water. It was a real Viking funeral. And if ever a tadpole deserved such a send-off, it was Timmy.

He was one tough tadpole.

—30—

And I Feared a Shotgun Wedding

SEX WAS OF GREAT interest for me from the first moment I noticed there was a difference between boys and girls. Despite this, I managed to reach the age of eleven without understanding the fine points of human reproduction.

Don't laugh. It really wasn't funny. In fact, I don't know how the truth eluded me for so long. It was a combination of things, I guess, arising from the conspiracy of silence perpetrated by neo-Puritans, especially in the South, in the years following World War II.

Parents who couldn't discuss the subject, a lack of available textbooks, and the assumption by peers who did know that everyone else was also well informed conspired to keep even a literate child with above-average intelligence, who had watched farm animals reproducing since his early years, from understanding the process.

The mechanics of human sexuality I understood perfectly well. When I was eight or nine, I found a set of outdated medical texts that had been abandoned in an illegal dump on the unpaved end of Rifle Range Road. I don't know how

195

old the books were, but they must have been from the turn of the century.

The sections on human sexuality talked about the harm of masturbation and ways to prevent nocturnal emissions, such as an admonition never to let little boys wear tight shorts to bed. That chapter, coupled with the fact that my father had once pointed out a retarded man as an example of what happened to those who practiced excessive masturbation, gave me worries about that for years to come.

It wasn't a scare tactic. My father believed it.

The old medical books had graphic drawings and photographs of human sexual equipment, including organs ravaged by venereal diseases. I learned the names of all the various parts and what part fit where. Not that I needed that information. After all, I had seen French postcards with dusky, Moorish-appearing women and light-skinned European men disinterestedly copulating for the photographer.

The connection I failed to make was the one between sexual intercourse and reproduction. Silly as it sounds now, no book of the hundreds I had ever read (including *Peyton Place* in snatched moments at the house of one of my aunts) ever said: *To accomplish pregnancy, insert penis into vagina and inject semen.*

Do you see? I even knew that the union of sperm and egg produced an embryo. *I simply had not made a connection between sexuality and reproduction.* Or to be more precise, how the sperm and egg got together. I thought sex was something that everyone practiced in secret—but just for fun.

Pregnancy, on the other hand, held romantic and mystic intonations for me. A man and woman, in my childish version of reproduction, had to be passionately and intimately involved. It was a thing that mysteriously happened when people hugged and kissed a lot, just like in the true confession magazines I would sneak and read when we visited my aunts. My father didn't allow them around our house.

Also, such a scenario made sense to me because it was the young lovers, kissing, hugging, and holding hands, who had babies—not people of my parents' age who had been married for years.

At the age of eleven, when I had my first romantic fling, at least the first that included physical activity, I was not prepared for the repercussions of the encounter.

Mary was not beautiful, but her eyes got me the first time I saw her. Mary was a year younger, which made her a precocious ten. She moved into our neighborhood in the middle of a school year.

I didn't see her arrive, though I watched the movers unload her belongings. The next morning, however, when I got on the bus, she was there, sitting two seats back. Tiny, with unruly blond hair, slightly crooked front teeth, wearing a pleated skirt and a white blouse, she was not extraordinary looking, until she saw me staring at her and smiled.

The smile completely changed her. To me, it was like the sudden appearance of the sun in the morning. With uncharacteristic boldness, I walked to her seat and stood by it. She slid over without saying a word, as if she had been waiting for me all her life. I was so entranced that the giggles and snickering of my peers meant nothing.

By the end of the week, we were holding hands on the bus and passing love notes back and forth at lunch. The second week, Mary had her mother call my mother to invite me over. My mother graciously said that Larry, my younger brother, and I could both visit. Even that did not cool my excitement.

Upon arrival, Mary's mother set out cookies and Kool-Aid. When we were finished, Mary told her we were all going down to the barn to play "house." I glanced quickly at my new love, looking for signs of humor. After all, "playing" was for small children, not big kids with romantic relationships. But she showed no sign that anything unusual was happening, and neither did her mother.

At the barn, actually a shed in the back yard, Mary quickly organized things. She turned my brother and her brother into the "children" and promptly put them out to play. They were no sooner out of sight than she turned and walked toward me slowly. Without warning, she put her arms around my neck and gave me my very first real kiss. It was sloppy, sweet, lingering and, above all, breathtaking.

"Did you like that?" she asked, looking up at me with an expression that managed to be impish and sophisticated at the same time.

"Yes," I croaked, without hesitation, in a voice that was already changing. I was her slave from that moment on until she abandoned me for an older man with a motorbike.

"I've been watching my sister [a high school girl] and her boyfriend. They do this all the time, especially out in the car at night. They do other things too. It's called neckin' and pettin'," she told me, once more pulling my face down to her. I was a willing student of whatever she wanted to teach me.

The next few weeks were glorious. On occasions when my mother allowed me to visit and at other times when my mother had no idea I was visiting, we played Mary's version of house, practicing and perfecting our techniques.

It was really harmless play that never went beyond a few daring peeks and forbidden touches, because even at that tender age—ignorant as I was of procreation—I knew that a "gentleman," especially a southerner, didn't ask the girl he was going to marry one day to "go all the way." The gossip columnists had always made that perfectly clear.

I don't know how many weeks our relationship went on before the thought struck me one night—like a bolt from the heavens—since we were *acting* like married people, fondling, kissing, hugging, and clinging to each other, the mysterious and mystic event just might happen to us. I shuddered at the thought that Mary might come to me at any time and say, "I've got some bad news . . ."

Horror washed over me at the very thought. We had been indiscreet, had taken the prerogatives of married people upon ourselves! Would it end in disgrace? Would they send Mary off to a home for unwed mothers? Or would her father stand behind me with a shotgun while the preacher sneeringly pronounced us a miniature man and wife?

The next few days I found myself looking from the corner of my eye at Mary's tummy and tiny cupcake breasts. The outdated medical text, my only source of real information on pregnancy, talked of swelling abdomens and enlarged breasts.

I made countless vows to stop all the hugging and kissing and petting, but I didn't have the strength. Looking back, I now know that a few words to Mary and my terror would have ended. It would, of course, have ended with peals of laughter at my expense, because I am certain that she knew the details.

It was my duty, as I saw it, to endure the worry and not bother my loved one with the horrible specter of social disgrace—fearing even to contemplate the consequences of what my father was apt to do when he found out that I had lied to him.

One afternoon during that period, noticing Mary and me walking hand in hand from the bus stop, my father, still in his work clothes, had bluntly asked: "You're not messin' around with that little girl, are you?" *Messin' around* was the euphemism my father always used for all sexual activity.

I hotly and emphatically denied it—telling the truth without being aware of it—but my heart pounded even harder when I thought about that conversation. I knew how my father felt about fornicators and adulterers.

Weeks of nightmares followed, until finally, when I could endure it no longer, I went to one of my school colleagues for advice.

If Mary was pregnant, I intended to do the right thing by her, whatever that might be, but I needed counsel.

If there had been a single adult with whom I could have comfortably discussed sex, or a good book on the subject, the agony that I endured would have been avoided. But there wasn't.

When I finally sought advice, it was from a classmate who had been held back two or three years. I remember that he was a fairly bright boy, who had somehow fallen between the cracks, suffering perhaps from a learning disorder not yet identified in the late 1950s. Or maybe he was just lazy. Twenty years later, I found him pumping gas, perfectly happy with his lot in life.

I figured that a man of his age and experience would be sympathetic to my problem.

Taking him aside on the playground one afternoon, I simply blurted it out. "I think my girlfriend's pregnant. How can I tell for sure?"

He looked at me, lifting on eyebrow. "Did she *tell* you that?" he asked.

"No."

"Then what makes you think she's pregnant?" He was responding just like I knew a man of fourteen would respond—concern, but no condemnation.

"Well . . . we've been . . . you know . . . messin' around." I fell back on my father's term.

"Oh," he appeared genuinely surprised. "You've started early. I didn't have sex the first time until I was about thirteen." He watched me closely for signs of doubt on my part.

Sex? Suddenly I was confused. I had asked about pregnancy and he was talking to me about sex.

"Haven't you been usin' a rubber?" he asked.

"No." I was staring at him, stunned from the turn the conversation had taken.

"You really ought to. I admit it ain't as much fun when you wear one," he was no doubt speaking from long years of experience, "but if them little sperms can't get out and swim up inside a girl, there sure ain't no way for her to get pregnant."

As the import of his words sank in, synapses began to close in the depths of my pubescent mind. *Sex was the direct cause of pregnancy!* How had I not seen it before? Then, almost in the same moment, relief began to wash over me like the ocean over a beach at high tide.

Mary was not pregnant. I would not be disgraced before the members of Union Baptist Church. Mary's father would not stand behind me with a shotgun while the minister sneered at me. Best of all, I had learned the awesome truth without having to admit that, until just moments before, I hadn't known what caused pregnancy.

"Well, how can I tell for sure if she's pregnant?" I had to continue the sessions or admit my folly of moments before.

"Well, until her belly swells up like a pumpkin, I guess. The only way you'll know for sure is if she tells you that her period's late."

"I really appreciate you takin' the time to help me out," I told him.

"No problem. You need to know about anything else, feel free to ask. That's why I'm here."

My heart sang for the rest of the day. A great burden had been lifted from my soul. I could hardly wait to get back to necking and petting with Mary.

Unfortunately, the relationship ended shortly thereafter, torn asunder by an older man on a moped.

—31—

The Ripsnorting Hunter

I NEVER MET AN even-tempered member of the Hunter clan. There have been a few through the years who have pretended to be mild mannered and civilized, but it's always a show. Hit the right button and you will see their true color emerge. That color is red.

The Berlands, my paternal grandmother's people, were excitable French-Canadians. Whenever my father wanted to make his mother angry, he would call her a "Canuck," or he would tell her that the French were a bunch of pansies who sold their country out to Hitler because they were afraid to fight.

This would bring on a fit of rage, replete with bilingual cursing, which no one else understood. Mam-maw Hunter had not learned English until the age of twelve and had refused to teach her children French because she had encountered so much difficulty in the Kansas school system where she learned to read.

My Grandfather Hunter, descended from the Scots who had settled in Tennessee looking for privacy, was even more ill-tempered than the Berlands. He would fight at the drop

203

of a hat, and he was notorious for it, even in Cocke County, Tennessee, once noted for a number of less-than-peaceful and law-abiding citizens.

Legend has it that the Cocke County sheriff and several deputies once broke up a bar fight and were leading arrestees to the cars. Noticing a man hiding under the steps, the sheriff is supposed to have said, "Come on, you're under arrest."

"I ain't comin' out until you chain up that sawed-off little bald-headed devil," the man allegedly replied in reference to my grandfather. Like most of the rest of us, William Franklin Hunter was not very tall.

As you can see, the descendants of Laura and Frank Hunter had almost no chance at a calm disposition.

My Baptist deacon father asked God every day in his prayers for help controlling himself, but God apparently left him with a "thorn in the flesh," like the apostle Paul.

The day after suffering a stroke, which paralyzed one side of his body, my father managed to punch out a rude and careless orderly with his one good arm. After that, all of the hospital personnel were wary of offending him, even though he was near death—or so the doctors thought at the time.

All the members of the clan, at least the ones I knew, were mercurial, but my Uncle Emery, my father's older brother, had a unique feature. It was a built-in alarm. If you were alert, it was possible to escape until he cooled off.

Emery was taller than most members of the family. He was barrel-chested and, like most of us, had a Roman nose (my father said such noses were called that because they "roamed" all over our faces). Uncle Emery turned very red in the face when he became upset, but his alarm system was more than a flushed face. He snorted when he was losing his temper. As his breathing grew deeper, great gasps of air caused a reverberation somewhere deep in his throat. It was a lot like the noise made by an angry bull just before it charges. If you entered the house and heard what sounded like an angry bull, it was best to flee the premises.

Emery Hunter was a remarkable man. Having been forced to quit school and go to work just after completing the seventh grade, he nevertheless managed to rise to executive rank with a major insurance company. He was a good provider, took pride in his work, and loved his children.

Unfortunately, he fell heir to the curse, handed down from both sides of his family. I was about eleven when I first saw his alarm system in operation.

It had been a pleasant Saturday afternoon, a family day. Uncle Emery's boys, Mike, Gary, and Edwin, had a large wading pool, about two feet deep. The three of them, my brother Larry, and I had been splashing in it all day. Being the eldest, I had led the group in various adventures. We had been everything from navy frogmen to pilots lost on a raft at sea.

Our mothers were in the house preparing for an outdoor cookout—tomatoes, potato chips, pickles. Dad sat in a lawn chair, talking to Uncle Emery, who was grilling steaks and hamburgers on a portable charcoal grill.

"You boys get dressed. We'll be ready to eat in a few minutes," Uncle Emery said.

We trooped into the house, dribbling water behind us, and toweled off. At some point during the dressing stage, Mike, who was about ten, and Gary, around eight, became involved in an argument.

By the time we were all dressed, the argument had degenerated into a fight. Gary, practicing discretion, began to retreat. We all followed them outside, shouting instructions to both of them. A fight was not a thing to be missed.

Down the front steps and around to the side Gary ran, stopping just at the corner. He picked up a loose brick, once stored under the house but dragged out and left by sloppy boys. As Mike rounded the corner, Gary bashed him on the head.

Stunned, Mike took a few staggering steps, then fell over. A lump and small cut were visible on his sunburned scalp, through his blond crewcut.

We all stood, momentarily paralyzed at the sight of the knot on Mike's head and the blood.

"He asked for it," Gary said defensively, apparently realizing the enormity of his crime. Someone, Larry, I think, ran to get Uncle Emery, telling him the story on the way back.

By the time Emery stalked around the side of the house, already red in the face, spatula in hand, Mike was sitting up, holding his head.

"Did you hit your brother in the head with a brick?" Emery demanded to know, as if unable to believe it.

Gary nodded his head.

"Why would you do such a thing?" his father asked, a small snort, not loud, but distinct, escaping his throat.

"You told me," Gary said, "that if anyone bigger than me jumped on me, that I should pick up anything I could find and bust 'em with it. That's what I did."

"I didn't tell you . . . (snort) . . . to kill . . . (snort)" Emery was advancing, waving the spatula "—your own flesh and blood . . . (snort) . . . Did I?"

Gary moved quickly, but he had ignored the snorting too long. Uncle Emery got in three or four swift blows across Gary's behind with the flat of the spatula before he could escape, then he turned to where Mike had been lying—but he had already fled the scene at the first loud snort.

There was a subdued bunch of boys that evening.

I was not on hand for Uncle Emery's most dramatic snorting fit several years later, but I have heard it told often. Gary was also at the heart of this story, though not the offender.

About thirteen at the time, Gary had become embroiled in a dispute with a young man of eighteen or so. Seeing the dispute, Emery charged out of the house in his long, baggy boxer shorts. Those shorts always intrigued me. Most military veterans never wore anything but jockey shorts after escaping from uniformity, but Uncle Emery had stuck with the more colorful style.

Intervening in the dispute, he showed remarkable restraint, especially for a member of our family. "You need to find someone your own size to fight with," he warned.

"How about you, old man?" the foolhardy youth retorted, as he threw a punch at Uncle Emery.

The young man, apparently unaware of what the snorting meant, stood there sneering while the irate Emery seized the first thing that came to hand, a small baseball bat that was lying in the yard. Seeing the weapon, the youth fled.

For blocks they ran, Uncle Emery in his brightly colored boxer shorts, T-shirt, and black socks, swinging the bat at the retreating bully, yelling, "Try to hit an old man again, you little SOB!"

Eventually the young man got away. Youth and terror probably saved him. I know it saved Mike and me the time we left the lid off a gallon of white paint. Reaching up to get it from the shelf where we had left it earlier in the day, Uncle Emery poured it all over his head. Mike and I were over the back fence before the first snort ended.

He had an alarm, but you had to pay attention.

lies like Bobby. I could have walked by this house forever and never stopped.

"Tell me what you're selling," she said with a smile when I returned with my papers. Her lipstick was a bright red, I noticed.

"Well, it's called *Grit* . . . there's something for everybody . . . sports, cartoons . . . all kinds of good stuff." I had a carefully prepared spiel, but it had left me. My tongue seemed to have turned to wood.

"How much is it?" she asked.

"Fifteen cents," I replied. I would have gladly given her the entire stack.

"Finish your Coke and I'll get the money."

I watched her leave, then looked around. The place had the neatness of a hotel lobby. To me, it looked luxurious. On the table beside the couch was a picture of Mrs. Jones and a much older man with silver hair.

"Is this your father?" I asked as she returned.

"No. That's my husband, Frank Jones. My name is Lela." She handed me a quarter. "I don't have any change, so just keep it all."

Even at the age of eleven, I knew I had committed a faux pas with my remark about her "father." She silenced me with a wave of her hand as I tried to stammer out an apology.

"That's all right," she smiled. "Older people than you make the same mistake. Mr. Jones is a nice man, and I married him when I was very young."

As she escorted me to the front door, I noticed for the first time that her toenails were painted the same shade as her lips. She was elegance personified, and I was totally smitten.

From that moment on, I began to live for the day that my *Grit* newspapers came. Every day I covered my school papers with hearts inscribed "Lela," though I always called her "Mrs. Jones" in person.

One day, when I was grown (the fantasy went), I would knock on her door. She would be overwhelmed when she saw me in my Marine Corps dress blues and her heart would pound. I would carry her away from the clutches of the evil old man to whom she was married.

I had convinced myself that he had somehow tricked her into matrimony and was holding her against her will. After all, she was young and beautiful and he was ancient, at least forty years old, maybe even older.

None of this I told Mrs. Jones, though I put my first passionately written love sonnets anonymously in her mailbox. Once I even bought and mailed a flowery "sweetheart" card to her—without return address, of course.

She never embarrassed me, though I am certain she knew the identity of her secret admirer. Each week she purchased a paper and paid me with a quarter. Most of the time, she would set out a Coke for me. I would drink it and cast surreptitious glances at her, depressed by the fact that it would be a week before I saw her again.

I began to seriously neglect my schoolwork and my friends.

"Come on," Johnny Clark said. "I promise you ain't never seen nothin' like this before."

"What is it?" I asked, showing little interest. Johnny lived a mile from me, up near the rifle and pistol range that gave Rifle Range Road its name. There was also an archery range.

"I ain't gonna tell you. I'm the only one who knows about it. You'll be the second one."

"Oh, all right. I'll tell my momma we're gonna play ball at your house."

All neighborhood children were strictly forbidden to play in or around the rifle and archery ranges because it was posted No Trespassing and because it was a notorious lovers lane, not to mention the razor-sharp arrows we sometimes found in the underbrush.

"Come on, let's hurry. He'll be there by three-thirty," Johnny urged.

"Who will?"

"Just wait and see," he replied mysteriously.

We entered from the side, sliding under the ineffective

fence that had been erected to keep out nonmembers. The archery range was a maze of paths meandering through several acres of woodland. At various points, paper targets with different animal shapes were mounted on bales of straw.

No member ever knew those woods the way neighborhood children did. On numerous occasions, they had tried to scare us off, but it did no good. We were like rabbits eluding dogs. Sometimes we would let them chase us a while, just for the fun of it, but when we were ready to end it, it ended.

There were a thousand places to hide if you were small and if you knew where they were.

"Where are we goin'? You can at least tell me that."

"You know that dead end at the very back?" His desire to talk about the secret finally overcame his desire to surprise me.

"Yeah?"

"You know Bobby, the high school guy that drives the old maroon Ford?"

"Yeah."

"Well, he's been there every day this week with a girl," Johnny said breathlessly.

"So?"

"I've watched 'em do it twice now."

"No kiddin'? You saw *everything*?" Johnny suddenly had my undivided attention.

"Everything. I saw her tits both times, and once I got a good look between her legs when she was puttin' her panties back on. She turned around with the door open."

"Let's hurry," I said. Never had I seen a naked woman, except in *National Geographic*, *Playboy*, and a stack of French postcards brought back from Europe by the father of one of my friends. *National Geographic* and *Playboy* obviously did not count since they fostered the illusion that women had no pubic hair.

"He's already here," Johnny whispered. "I hope we ain't missed it."

Silently we approached the old Ford. I was afraid the occupants would hear my breath hissing in and out, even inside the vehicle. Approaching the passenger side, Johnny stood and peeked in.

"Go to the other side," Johnny hissed. "She's on top today."

Duck-walking, I made my way around to the passenger side, suddenly aware of grunts and moans coming from inside. The heavy car was shaking slightly.

Taking a deep breath, I raised up and peered through the back-seat window. A female figure, sitting astride her partner, suddenly sat up and leaned backward, eyes closed and mouth open, slowly undulating on her partner. Her arms were crossed over her breasts as she hugged herself in apparent ecstasy.

I recognized her! The shock went through me like ice water through my heart. Then she opened her eyes and saw me. She grimaced slightly but did not scream or speak. It was my love goddess, Lela Jones.

A moment later I was running full speed through the woods, tears stinging my eyes. Betrayed! Not with a movie star, not with a secret agent, not even with a U.S. Marine in dress blues—but with a greasy-haired high school punk who got his kicks by spraying younger kids with a water hose.

When I was sure that Johnny could not catch up with me, I sat down and cried. My love goddess, the first older woman in my life, was soiled beyond recovery. Only later did I realize that although Bobby had enjoyed carnal knowledge of her, Johnny had seen her naked and I had been denied even that because her arms had been in the way. It was a bitter pill to swallow.

Months later, she was at her mailbox as I walked down the road on my way to a back-yard football game. I had no intention of speaking to the woman who had so thoroughly betrayed me. Nevertheless, my heart began to chug when I saw her.

"David, I want to talk to you about what you saw."

"I'm not gonna tell anybody." I started to walk around her, but she blocked my way.

"I didn't think you would," she said quietly.

"I don't have to. Bobby'll do that," I said, tears once more welling in my eyes. "I've heard him before." The bitterness suddenly poured out of me. "He brags about all the girls he's had. How could you do that with him? He's . . . he's . . . ignorant and loud!"

Indeed he was and so he remained. Nearly twenty-five years later, when I arrested him for drunk driving, he still had the ducktail and a souped-up hot rod.

There were tears in her eyes as she smiled at me sadly. "Go on, David, you're not ready to understand yet. Maybe someday you will. Try not to think too badly of me."

It was the last time I ever saw her. A few months later, the house was vacant. Lela Jones was wrong, though. All these years later, I still don't understand.

Not with him.

— 33 —

Childhood's End

*P*RIMITIVE TRIBES the world over have rites of passage, initiations into adulthood. They vary from tribe to tribe; sometimes they are painful and frightening, sometimes not. Whatever the initiation, though, when it is over, the new member is an adult with full rights and benefits.

Our society, I think, would benefit from such a rite of passage. As it is, young people are left in limbo for too many years, thrashing violently about for acceptance. We suffer from prolonged periods of apprehension, from protracted periods of youth.

When I sat down to write about my childhood from the inside out, I was not sure where the book would end. At what point did my childhood cease? When did the pristine view of life become corrupted with the poisons of adult worries?

For me, I have discovered, childhood withered away in my eleventh year, not with a bang, but a whimper. Puberty had me in its grip; I received my last spanking and my last toy pistol. Worst of all, though, I found out what Christmas had really cost my parents through the years.

★　★　★

217

"Come on," Larry said. "I'm never gonna learn to ride a big bicycle, if you don't help me." He spoke with the determination of a cotton-topped eight-year-old.

"Dad says you're too small for this bicycle. Ride your own," I told him.

"I wanna learn to ride *this* one. I'm nine years old."

"Ya'll better do what Daddy says or he'll bust ya." Pat piped in. At six, she was not shy about expressing her opinion, though she knew we would ignore her. Being the youngest and the only female is not easy, I guess.

"All right," I said, "but if you get hurt, I've had it."

"Daddy'll bust ya both," Pat said again.

"Daddy ain't even here," Larry snapped. "Besides, when he sees me ridin' this twenty-six-inch bike, he'll be so surprised that he won't care."

"Wait and see," Pat warned, flouncing away. "He'll bust both of you—good and hard."

Spankings were not routine at our house but were reserved for serious offenses, such as life-threatening acts or lying, and they were administered on the culprit with incredible speed.

Larry and I usually fared better than Pat did. As soon as the first blow fell (and sometimes before) both of us would begin to yell for mercy.

Pat, however, had a streak of stubbornness that was incredible. She would endure a spanking without flinching. Once, after she wrote on the walls with crayons, Larry said that he had done it and was spanked for it. Upon finding out (I think I was the snitch) that Larry had been unfairly punished, Dad called Pat in and told her to apologize to him.

She refused, even after several spankings and threats of a horrible nature. I don't remember if she ever did give in and say she was sorry.

"Mind your own business!" Larry yelled to her retreating back. "I can learn to ride this big bicycle."

"You're gonna get busted!" she called back one more time.

"All right," I told him. "I'm gonna run alongside you and

hold onto the seat. If you get hurt, I *will* get busted. Don't try to ride away from me."

"I won't," Larry promised.

In a few moments, he was precariously perched high on the seat of the twenty-six-inch English-style bike. His legs barely reached the pedals. As we circled the house, I helped him maintain his balance.

He could ride his own bike well. But mounting and dismounting from the tall bike were beyond him. Within a few minutes, he was cruising smoothly along.

"Turn loose," he said. "I've got it."

"No. I don't want you to fall over. It's time to stop. I'm tired."

"One time. Let me take it around one time by myself," he implored.

"No. It's time to stop."

"Just once," he pleaded again, as we were rounding the house to the front yard.

"All right. *One time.*" I stopped to catch my breath and watched him wobble on.

Our father pulled into the driveway at that very moment. I saw him and Larry saw him. That was probably what startled Larry and caused him to lose control, heading downhill directly toward a head-on collision with the 1953 maroon and yellow Packard that was Dad's pride and joy. Dad braked hard and stopped.

Wobbling from side to side, fighting hard for control, Larry narrowly missed the grill of the Packard. The front wheel of the bicycle hit one of the large white river rocks lining the driveway and twisted sideways, hurling Larry to the ground.

I watched in horror as the scene nightmarishly unfolded. Larry rose from the wreckage, rubbing his leg. As Dad rounded the front of the Packard, Larry forgot his leg and ran about four paces, then realizing the folly of his actions, he stopped and gritted his teeth.

Dad examined him for injuries, and finding nothing serious, began to whack him across the behind, talking as he did. I could not hear the words as I stood frozen in place, but I knew I would hear them when my time came.

He released Larry and came after me. Like Larry, I resisted the urge to run. During my childhood, I never had occasion to find out just what the penalty for running away from a spanking was. I never had the nerve to try it.

"I told you . . . (whack!) . . . not to let your little brother . . . (whack!) . . . ride the big bicycle! (whack!) You almost killed him. (whack!) Don't ever . . . (whack!) do it again! (whack!) And I . . . (whack!) *mean* it." Moments into the spanking, I was yelling for mercy.

He turned me loose and went on into the house, muttering about children with no common sense at all. Larry limped across the yard, pushing the big bike. Pat came out on the front porch and propped her bare foot up on the bottom of the railing.

"I said ya'd get busted, didn't I?"

It was my last spanking ever, though I had no way of knowing it at the time.

"What do you boys want for Christmas?" our father asked, sitting down on our bed.

"I want a six-gun that you can fan the hammer on and load bullets in," Larry said. The "fanner pistol" was all the rage that year. Some television cowboy hero, the Sundance Kid or Johnny Ringo maybe, had a pistol that could be fired by merely hitting the hammer or "fanning it." The toy manufacturers had picked it up.

Toy guns had always been a staple of Christmas at our house. There was a new set every year, and usually a cowboy hat and boots to go with them. Our father was, I believe, buying the things that he had always wanted as a child, but never got.

He overdid Christmas, because his own childhood memories were so shabby. I was about to find out what Christmas had really cost him through the years.

"What about you, David?"

"I dunno. Some clothes, I guess."

"Yeah, I guess you are gettin' too old for toys," he conceded, perceiving what was going through my mind. "You'll be in junior high school before you know it."

"Yep," I said.

"I was just thinkin', though, maybe you'd like to have one more cowboy pistol—since this will be the last year."

"Yeah," I brightened. "I guess *one more* wouldn't hurt—since it'll be the last year."

I was greatly relieved.

"Come on," Dad said not many days later. "Let's go for a ride."

"Can I go?" Larry asked, jumping up from the floor in front of the television.

"No. I need your brother to help me with somethin'."

Outside in the old Packard I noticed the things on the front floorboard. There was an electric drill, an electric skill saw, an expensive wrench set, and Dad's .22 caliber Ruger target pistol. I had seen him load them in the car before, just prior to his many trips out of town looking for work.

I had never asked why. Though we had never lived in luxury, we had never lacked a necessity. A few minutes later on that December day, as we stopped in front of the pawn shop, I realized for the first time where he had been taking his valuables on days just before he made out-of-town trips.

As I helped my father carry the things into the pawn shop, a horrible reality came over me: the source of our coming Christmas celebration was about to be revealed.

The man behind the window cataloged my father's personal items, then counted out money to him. I watched, stunned, as the items were placed on the shelves in back. We were outside in the car before Dad spoke.

"Do you know how pawn shops work?"

"I . . . I think so." I remember staring at the floorboard in shame.

"When I have more money, I'll go back and get my things. The pawn shop charges money to loan money."

I sat, still not able to look at the man who had just pawned his most precious belongings so his children could have a nice Christmas.

"I didn't let you see this to make you feel bad," he said. "I just thought it was time you knew how tough the world can be when you're poor and don't have an education. We're better off this year than we usually are. I didn't have to go to the finance company and borrow money for Christmas this year. When you don't have an education, son, you do the best you can."

It all rushed in on me with a horrible, gut-wrenching clarity. I understood why my parents only bought each other token gifts. I understood why winter was always such a time of stress. Ironworkers could only work when the weather permitted, because most ironwork is done outside.

My parents would put away money when it was good weather and hope that the out-of-work time in the winter would not be too long. When it was really bad, my father would pawn his personal belongings and go to Cincinnati or Dayton—with only enough cash to get him there.

And at Christmas my parents would borrow money so that we would have presents piled high under the tree.

"We're gonna take this money and go shoppin'," Dad said that afternoon as we left the pawn shop. "Christmas is next week."

At Grant's Department Store, we found Larry's six-gun with the "fanning hammer and bullets that you load." There were also assorted small toys for him. For my sister, there was the traditional doll and dish set and other little-girl things.

"Have you found the gun you want, yet?" my father asked.

"No, I'm still lookin'."

"What about that one?" It was an exact replica of a real Old West six-gun (a Remington, I think), with all the working parts, down to the removable cylinder.

"Naw, it's too expensive," I said, aware for the first time in my life of exactly what "expensive" meant.

"No, I think a boy's last cap pistol ought to be the best."
He picked it up and dropped it in the basket. I flatly refused

to pick out anything else, knowing that the one pistol was the price of his prized electric drill. He did not press the point but went back and bought other items for me when I was not with him.

The memory of that Christmas is bittersweet. Vaguely I was beginning to understand that my father, who could not say, "I love you," because he had never learned how, *did* love me.

In the years to come, in the storms of adolescence and young manhood, I would lose track of that knowledge at times. There would be bitterness between my father and me, as two stubborn individuals went at loggerheads to each other.

He would accuse me of being a "fuzzy-headed dreamer," unable to function in the real world. My poetry, books, and love of art he could not understand; his antagonism to my goals, I could not tolerate.

We were both wrong—and right. I *was* a "fuzzy-headed dreamer," with a rough road ahead of me for many years. I did survive, though, and with most of my dreams intact. Had he lived, I think he would have been proud of what I have accomplished.

My eleventh Christmas was the beginning of my understanding of life as it really is. Sadly, the beginning of understanding also heralded childhood's end.

David Hunter has written four books of police stories and two mystery novels—*The Moon Is Always Full, Black Friday Coming Down, The Jigsaw Man, There Was Blood on the Snow, The Night Is Mine,* and *Homicide Game*—all of which grew out of his experiences as an investigator with the Knox County, Tennessee, sheriff's department. His books have been described as full of "adventure, excitement, laughter, tears, compassion, indignation, and nobility." In this book, one of Tennessee's most popular storytellers has turned his talents toward exploring those events of his early life that shaped him and a generation. In doing so, David Hunter tells poignant tales that will touch your heart and stir your memories.